Be Seated

Published by Applied Research and Design Publishing, an imprint of ORO Editions.
Gordon Goff: Publisher

www.appliedresearchanddesign.com
info@appliedresearchanddesign.com

Text and drawings by Laurie Olin
Photographs by Olin and as credited
Project Coordinator: Kirby Anderson

Graphic Design: Pablo Mandel / www.circularstudio.com
Typeset in URW Geometric and Minion Pro

10 9 8 7 6 5 4 3 2 1 First Edition

Library of Congress data available upon request. World Rights: Available

ISBN: 978-1-939621-72-6

Color Separations and Printing: ORO Group Ltd.
Printed in China.

International Distribution: www.appliedresearchanddesign.com/distribution

ORO Editions makes a continuous effort to minimize the overall carbon footprint of its publications.
As part of this goal, ORO Editions, in association with Global ReLeaf, arranges to plant trees to
replace those used in the manufacturing of the paper produced for its books. Global ReLeaf is an
international campaign run by American Forests, one of the world's oldest nonprofit conservation
organizations. Global ReLeaf is American Forests' education and action program that helps
individuals, organizations, agencies, and corporations improve the local and global environment by
planting and caring for trees.

Be Seated
Laurie Olin

a r + d

APPLIED
RESEARCH
+DESIGN
PUBLISHING

For Victoria

Contents

Introduction

Among the surviving 35 mm slides taken on my first heady trip to Paris as a young architect in 1967 are several portraits of chairs: a handsome verdigris metal chair in the Tuileries, a white one in an outdoor café in the same garden, a dark magenta one in the Bois de Boulogne. During that trip I also noticed (but didn't take photos of) others found throughout these parks made of simple metal frames with wooden slats, some with arms but most without. In those days rather fierce older women roamed the Tuileries and Luxembourg Garden collecting a fee for the use of each chair. It was a very small sum, only a few centimes. One could have the use of a rented chair—or several, if desired—until the park closed at the end of the day.

Like many in my generation, I went to Paris because its art, film, design, and literature had earned it the reputation of being one of the most culturally stimulating places in the world. I was not disappointed. But what I hadn't bargained on was how taken I would be with its cafés and parks and gardens—the urban spaces where the city's artists and designers and writers had met, read, dined, drunk, worked, and argued for decades. In fact everyone, locals and tourists alike, seemed to meet and spend time in these places.

I was especially struck by the simplicity of the design and fixtures that comprised the Parisian public realm. The tables, chairs, and terraces were sturdy and well made—elegant, even—yet also deceptively unobtrusive: simple pavements of gravel, asphalt, or stone; trees and umbrellas or awnings for shade and some weather protection; tables and chairs. Many of the squares that I liked the most—what the French call *places*—were clearly delineated outdoor rooms framed by buildings and streets and incorporating trees. The most striking examples were the Tuileries and the Palais Royal, but there were many smaller ones scattered throughout Montmartre and Saint-Germain. The *places* were generally defined by low walls, hedges, planters, changes in level, and a café. That was it. The ubiquity of chairs in these spaces allowed for a remarkable sociability in large portions of the public realm. And yet there was an ordinariness, a quotidian aspect to it, that belied their canny design and arrangement. This example of the humble chairs, tables, and park benches in Paris eventually came to contribute significantly to my attitude and design direction regarding civic space.

My growing interest in public places and how we occupy them was accompanied over the years by an equal interest in the issue of how varied the expression of a simple thing can be. I would point out the number of bridges in Philadelphia to my students and show how at least eight of them spanned the same distance and held up the weight of similar loads of traffic, yet they were all different in form and of several materials; all did their job, but some were handsome, some ugly, and some truly elegant. At some point chairs registered as another simple, nearly universal design problem with an

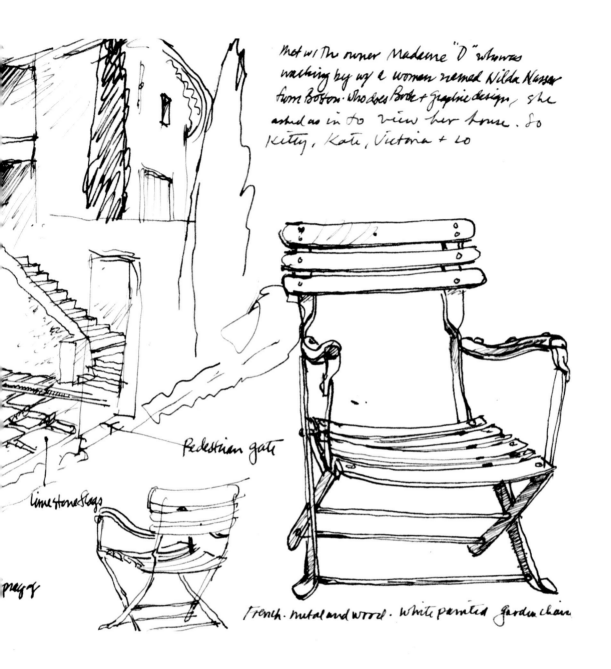

met w/ The owner Madame "D" who was
walking by w/ a woman named Nilda Nasser
from Boston. Who does Book + Graphic design, she
asked as in to view her house. So
Kitty, Kate, Victoria + Lo

Pedestrian gate

Lime Stone flags

peggy

French. metal and wood. White painted Garden chair

PREVIOUS PAGES The sketches on pages 5 and 6 are of men on Skid
Road in Seattle, from my book *Breath on the Mirror* (1972).

ABOVE Typical metal and wood chair found in the Tuileries and
Luxembourg Garden in Paris and throughout France. This example was
in a private garden in Provence and is heavier and sturdier than those
derived from it that have recently become common in American public
and private spaces. SB 83 pen and ink, 1991

extraordinary number of practical and aesthetic solutions. While working on these projects later, whether indoors or out, I was inevitably mulling over the question of seating. Each urban landscape project presented different challenges and possibilities.

Thinking back and leafing through my sketchbooks, I see that I've been looking at, studying, and recording furniture indoors and out for the past fifty years. On a fairly regular basis I have noted examples that interested me because of their form, proportions, dimensions, structure, and materials (or some combination that I found attractive or instructive) in places ranging from parks in Paris and Barcelona to cafés in Vienna and Bucharest, from villas in Italy to railroad stations in the American West. A number of successful landscape places I have admired and sketched, such as Paley Park in New York City, turn out to possess what amounts to built-in seating in the form of ledges or convenient walls as well as loose furniture.

It became clear to me that under certain circumstances people in public places would sit on just about anything, and in all manner of positions. In some instances this is desirable and has been consciously encouraged through the careful proportions, dimensions, and arrangement of planters, walls, stairs, and ledges. In the case of particularly well-designed public spaces, these inconspicuous details can both accommodate a substantial population when necessary and also contribute to a sense of well-being even when hardly anyone is present—unlike a stadium, for example, which can look abandoned and forlorn when empty. (Later I'll discuss efforts, on behalf of some, to discourage public use, as well as indicate the motives and results of attempting to make such utilitarian surfaces aggressively unpleasant—or even painful and dangerous.)

What follows begins with a history of seating in the landscape, followed by my own burgeoning fascination with public seating and a brief synopsis of how that fascination evolved. Next come thoughts gleaned from four decades of professional practice as a landscape architect in Europe and America, and my interest in chairs, benches, and experiments in contemporary projects. Finally, I include some brief reflections on public space and various aspects of its design. I have not attempted a comprehensive history or survey of seating; instead this is an appreciation derived from my personal observation of and frequent professional engagement with such arrangements—sometimes in gardens, but more particularly in public and civic environments.

Between and within the essays are a number of drawings and sketches that embody information about these subjects in a different—yet, I hope, equally rewarding—way. The drawings were not originally created as illustrations for a text but instead for myself over the span of many years, often while traveling and without any thought of sharing them. Some are quick, hasty notes; others are more careful studies, even on occasion measured. Some were made chiefly for pleasure while others represent an attempt to puzzle through a particular design problem. That is why they're not sprinkled through the essays like seasoning to improve the flavor of particular paragraphs as conventional illustrations sometimes are.

In many instances, though, they do exemplify something I am exploring in the preceding chapter. I therefore couldn't bear to relegate them to a monolithic block at the book's end in the irritating way that photos once accompanied art and architecture monographs—a practice done for reasons of cost that no longer prevail. Instead the drawings are in small clusters interleaved between the essays, or juxtaposed within the text to serve as an alternative presentation of the topics being discussed. This is the rhetorical strategy of a designer rather than that of a historian or critic. My hope is that it results in a dialogue between writing and image as well as between the images themselves.

It may baffle some readers that I have drawn and discussed examples of interior furniture—albeit not conclusively or separately—in a work that purports to be about outdoor seating. It isn't just that life is messy and I am disordered—although both those things are frequently true—but also that I am deeply interested in the world on both sides of the walls of our dwellings. Despite the current disciplinary limitations commonly thought of as architecture, landscape architecture, and interior design, life and behavior are unbounded; I see a continuum of activity from inside to out of doors. While sitting around for several decades I have learned that I can be just as comfortable or uncomfortable inside as out, and for years I have believed that lessons taken from one place might well help in another. This book is an attempt to share some of my thoughts on what that comfort depends upon.

My interest in outdoor seating in parks and plazas revolves around two poles: one is related to the fascination that Emerson and other philosophers have shown regarding aspects of the quotidian in our lives and experience, its pressures and benefits; the other is the utility of public seating in guiding our conduct as citizens. In a democracy we are expected to fulfill two potentials— that of a private citizen and that of a contributing member of a society. When sitting in a park or plaza, we are immersed in our private existence, with its particular demands and aspirations, while simultaneously participating in the larger, communal life of the town or city around us. Chairs and benches are the settings for this simple and largely unnoticed yet profoundly important aspect of our lives.

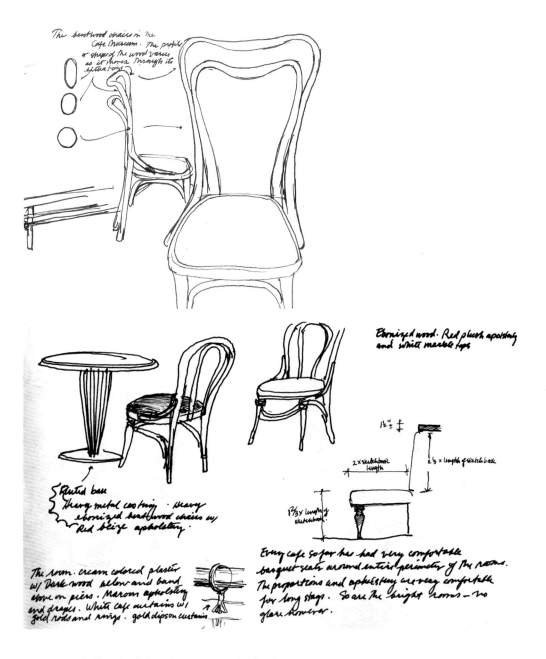

ABOVE, TOP Unlike Thonet's café chairs, this one in Prague has shaped
elements with variable width across the back in a manner one associates
with the style of Art Nouveau. SB 150, pen and ink, 2008

ABOVE, BOTTOM The classic Thonet café chair of bent beech wood,
sketched here in a café in Vienna along with a measured study of one of
the ubiquitous banquette seats found there in many cafés. SB 101, pen
and ink, 1995

LAURIE OLIN

BE SEATED

Jardin Luxembourg . 20 July 2003

ABOVE Afternoon in the Luxembourg Garden, where one can sit in any number of situations: either on one of the simple straight wooden benches developed and installed throughout the public spaces of Paris during the building boom of the Haussmann era, or on one of the familiar metal and wood chairs found everywhere in the park—along walks and terraces, under bosques and allées of trees. SB 134 watercolor, 2003

Thonet clerk claims they have no catalogue available and no U.S. dealers. One must order directly from Vienna.

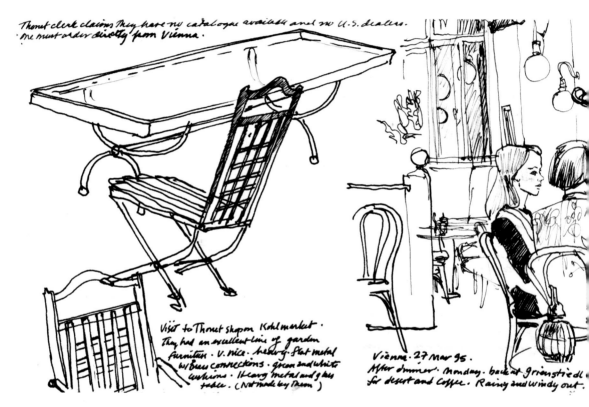

Visit to Thonet shop on Kohlmarket. They had an excellent line of garden furniture. V. nice. heavy. flat metal w/ brass connections. green and white cushions. Heavy metal and glass table. (Not made by Thonet)

Vienna. 27 Mar 95. After dinner. Monday. back at Grienstiedl for desert and coffee. Rainy and windy out.

Varieties of tables and chairs in Vienna: on the right, a classic
combination of a continuous banquette with small café tables and
Thonet chairs; on the left, contemporary garden furniture of metal and
glass in Thonet's salesroom. SB 101, pen and ink, 1995

LAURIE OLIN

Over the past forty years, the partners and staff in my office have sought to accommodate people and provide for their use, comfort, and stimulus in the many public and private spaces we have designed.[1] Occasionally we have collaborated with social scientists, craftsmen, and manufacturers, but more frequently we have drawn upon years of personal observation of human behavior and a familiarity with landscape furnishings and their use in public spaces in an almost encyclopedic array of places around the world. This professional habit has led to a great deal of experimentation in the design of seating, especially that of the most lowly type, benches. Although I have been a consistent advocate for moveable furnishings like tables and chairs, it has been the fixed elements—benches, steps, ledges, planters, and walls—commonly designed by landscape architects as part of the physical fabric of places to which I have devoted considerable energy. For it is these features that form the very bones of public landscapes, and that shape their use and character.

In the past two decades, growing interest on the part of many design firms, manufacturers, and public agencies has led to a noticeable increase in the amount and variety of exterior furnishings available. Often they have been imaginative, well designed, and handsomely made. Unfortunately there has also been a proliferation of much that is mediocre, as well as of formulas, rules, and ordinances legislating quantities of seating for public spaces. This has led to many instances where furnishings—especially seating—appear as so much clutter, visually and physically. In some cases, an excess of benches has transformed urban plazas into corrals: the unintended result of some bureaucratic attempt to achieve the prescribed amount of seating.

This proliferation of all-too-familiar industrial products has also contributed to a loss of particularity and local character. Just as the ubiquity of international corporate stores, highway design, and entertainment has led to a widespread loss of identity across America and elsewhere, bottom-line considerations are encouraging a mind-numbing uniformity in contemporary landscape design. While there is no guarantee of effective resistance to this phenomenon, the custom design of furnishings, when combined with a sensitivity to context and local conditions, can contribute significantly to community identity and a "sense of place."

---

1. The landscape architecture and urban design firm originally named Hanna/Olin, Ltd., founded in 1976, became the Olin Partnership in 1990 and has now evolved into the Olin Studio, also known simply as OLIN, with offices in Philadelphia and Los Angeles.

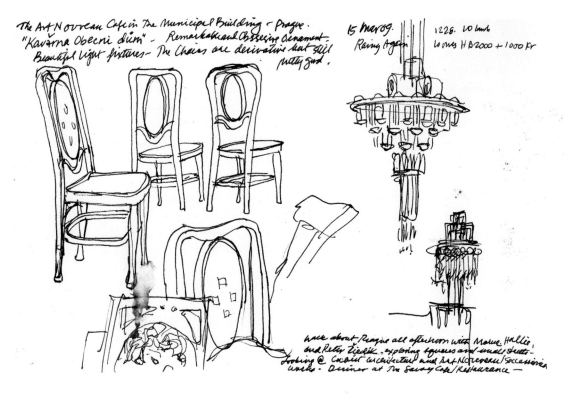

The Art Nouveau Cafe in The Municipal Building - Prague. "Kavárna Obecní dům" - Remarkable and Obsessive Ornament. Beautiful light fixtures - The Chairs are derivative but still pretty good.

15 Mar 09. Raing Again

1228. Lunch Looks HB 2000 + 1000 Kr

walk about Prague all afternoon with Marie, Hallie, and Peter Žiedik - exploring squares and small streets - looking @ Cubist architecture and Art Nouveau/Secessionist works - Dinner at The Savoy Cafe/Restaurance —

A variation on the bentwood café chair in an Art Nouveau-style café, Kavárna Obecní dům, in Prague. Although a bit stiff-looking and derivative, these chairs are both sturdy and comfortable. SB 150, pen and ink, 2008

Parc behind Notre Dame.
Isle de la Cité. Paris
21 Mar 2001

These simple benches of painted planks and iron frames, originally
developed in the 19th century as part of Adolphe Alphand's
transformation of the public realm, are located in the park behind Notre-
Dame Cathedral on the Île de la Cité, Paris. SB 125, watercolor, 2001

LAURIE OLIN

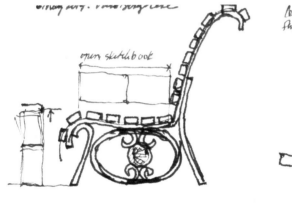

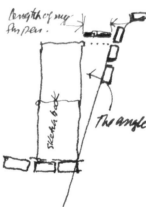

ABOVE TOP Exploring parks in Beijing, one encounters benches derived from those originally developed in the Mediterranean. This one was in a small park, originally a villa garden, on the campus of Tsinghua University. There are examples in many other public spaces in the city such as Beihai Park and the Temple of Heaven. SB 135, pen and ink, 2004

ABOVE BOTTOM Curious about the exact profile and angle of one of these benches, I made a measured drawing of this late-19th-century version in the park of the Villa Borghese, Rome. SB 160, pen and ink, 2014

OPPOSITE PAGE A classic profile that encourages lounging. At some point in the mid-19th century this bench first appeared in Barcelona and the south of France. Made of tropical hardwood dowels or slats mounted on a couple of cast-iron frames with legs set back from the ends, it was a perfect product for factory production, quick assembly, and installation, and it has spread around the world. Its lazy and seductive curves, especially in the double-sided version, make it as comfortable to linger upon as it looks. This example is in a public garden in Arles, France. SB 17, pen and ink, 1967

march · 1991 · Barcelona · Plaza Real · Lunch. gazpacho · Paella con Carne. vino Rosa. — Siesta

In the Plaça Reial in Barcelona one finds a felicitous mixture of benches
and chairs that allows for varied social use and relaxed behavior. SB 81,
pen and ink, 1991

LAURIE OLIN

24

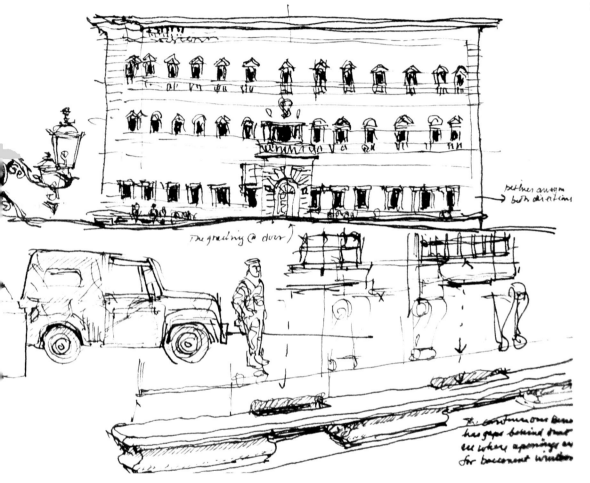

The graiding @ door)

sither arrage
both directions

The continuous seat
has gaps behind that
see where openings or
for basement windows

A continuous stone seat built into the base of Antonio da Sangallo's
Palazzo Farnese is often completely occupied from late afternoon into
the evening as it offers a shady seat and a privileged view of people
moving into and through the Piazza Farnese on their way to and from
the Campo de' Fiori, Rome. SB 160, pen and ink, 2014

LAURIE OLIN

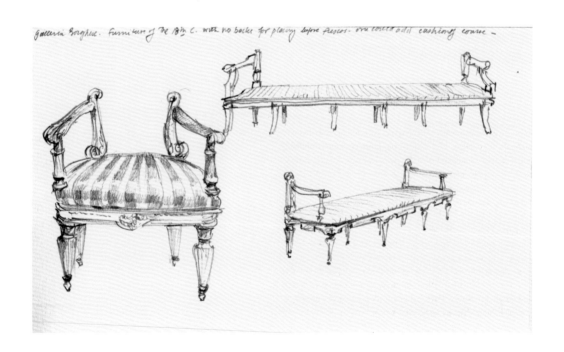

Galleria Borghese. Furniture of the 18th C. with no backs for placing before frescos. one could add cushions, coarse.

BE SEATED

maria della Consolazione - Todi. 23 Aug 1973 Up close one can't see the top, only the great undulating base on its plastform the neighborhood people come to sit about...

ABOVE Numerous ambitious Renaissance palazzos and churches offer seating to the public as part of the fabric of their structure, commonly in the form of a continuous stone ledge as the demarcation between a base molding or water-table and the wall. This example, with neighbors relaxing and chatting at the end of the day, is at the chapel of Santa Maria della Consolazione outside Todi in Umbria. SB 30, pen and ink, 1973

OPPOSITE While puzzling over these two examples of 17th-century furniture at the Villa Borghese—an elegant late rococo chair and bench—I suddenly realized the reason for the absence of a backrest. How was a person to sit in a chair or on a sofa if one was wearing a swallowtail coat or a voluminous dress or skirt with its structure of hoops, bustle, and train? Such parts of one's costume needed to be allowed to extend and fall behind what really amounted to a bench or stool. SB 123, graphite pencil, 1999

LAURIE OLIN

There are extensive histories of interior furniture—especially of what are called "antiques," valued today as examples of particularly fine design and craftsmanship—preserved and on display all over the globe. On visits to museums in Beijing, Rome, Cairo, and Tunis I have been stunned by encounters with Chinese, Egyptian, Greek, and Roman furniture from the past. Generally made of wood with metal fittings, these beds, tables, chairs, litters, and benches are often masterpieces of form and joinery, and among the most graceful objects I have ever encountered. Hundreds if not thousands of years old, many of them seem diminutive, intended as they were for people of smaller stature than most of the world's population today.

The functionality of a chair or bench has always interested me as much as its aesthetic appeal. Often when in a historic house or museum I wish that I could test out these pieces—to see how they really worked or felt, and if they were comfortable—and I wonder what the cushions that surely accompanied many of them were like. I also take pleasure in knowing that chairs and divans from the American Federal period were inspired by ancient Egyptian furnishings. (This is because, following Napoleon's expedition to Egypt, European designers and craftsmen began to incorporate Egyptian motifs, and an outpouring of fashionable pieces rapidly worked their way to the American market.) Although the American versions are often larger and heavier in proportion and structure than their European inspirations, I appreciate their elegance, and the connection they afford me to an ancient culture's habits of sitting.

All this furniture was made almost exclusively for interior use, however. Unsurprisingly, when it comes to outdoor seating, very few examples survive from the ancient world. In part this is because much of it was of wood or bronze with cloth and leather upholstery, and as such has rotted or been repurposed. Nevertheless, contemporary writings and visual records suggest that in private households some indoor seating—such as the ubiquitous folding stool with a cloth or leather seat—often served as outdoor seating as well, being carried outside with cushions by servants and slaves at certain times and seasons and then back indoors whenever appropriate. We know, for example, that privileged Romans reclined on *klinai*, or couches, to dine in open-air *triclinia*, outdoor loggias, and a variety of architectural pavilions. And then there are the curved, apsidal stone seats one sees in romantic paintings by Alma-Tadema and others that were based upon those found in Pompeii and other excavations. But all these would have been originally located within enclosed private gardens, palaces, memorials, and estates—whether Imperial or those of wealthy individuals.[2] What about seating in exterior public spaces?

OPPOSITE One of a pair of elegant wooden garden benches designed by William Kent, now in the orangery of a private estate in Ohio. Clearly intended to receive a flat pad for the seat and possibly loose cushions or throw pillows for the back, this relatively short bench invites intimate conversation and relations between two people. SB 110, pen and ink, 1997

2. Several of Lawrence Alma-Tadema's familiar paintings include semicircular marble benches with lion's leg arm rests similar to those of Karl Friedrich Schinkel's exedra bench at Charlottenhof in Berlin. These are quite obviously based upon benches at the tomb of Mamia in Pompeii that was discovered in 1769; a folio of prints of the ruins by Hackert and others was published and widely distributed in 1817.

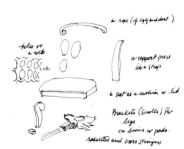

Chair by William Kent, one of a set of 16, at the Waxmans in New Albany.

The concept of assemblage: it is a collage of parts, elements and motifs, unblended but stuck together.

A Darwin chair, presented to Academy of Natural Sciences by his great grandson Nov 2, 1989. Originally at Down House, Kent, Darwin's family home

TOP RIGHT A chair by William Kent, one of a set of 16, private estate, Ohio, 1998. This nutty piece is quintessentially Kentissimo in composition in that it is an assemblage of various parts rounded up and stuck together according to the diagram for a chair, as is noted. SB 115, pen and ink, 1998

CENTER RIGHT A highly evolved English side chair, with a motif that can be seen as a sheaf of wheat, from Down House, the family home of Charles Darwin, presented to the Academy of Natural Sciences in Philadelphia by his granddaughter. SB 120, pen and ink, 1997

BOTTOM RIGHT Two 18th-century wooden chairs made in the English colonies of Massachusetts and Pennsylvania. One was intended to have cushions and prevent drafts upon the head, shoulders, and upper back of the user; the other was designed to contain a commode for convenient access. SB 120, pen and ink, 1999

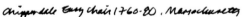

Chippendale Easy chair 1760-80. Massachusetts

Chester County commode chair. 1720-50

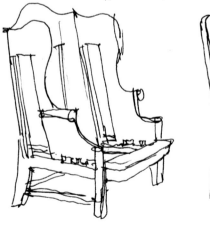

Famous exceptions have been the handsomely shaped and proportioned seats found in the surviving Greek and Roman theaters and gymnasia of antiquity; these have captured the attention of architects and designers for decades. Karl Friedrich Schinkel in the 19th century, Edwin Lutyens and Charles Adams Platt in the early 20th century, and modern masters such as Alvar Aalto, Le Corbusier, and Louis Kahn have all noted them—either in their sketchbooks or their architecture.

Less discussed, however, are the numerous resting places and benches that punctuated the circulatory routes of Roman cities. Throughout the Empire, in major and minor cities alike, there are remains of a variety of special places located along arterials and promenades that were furnished with steps, fountains, benches, arcades, and many examples of shade structures. William MacDonald, one of the most perceptive historians of classical urbanism and architecture, has pointed out that while the frequency of fountains adjacent to streets and at prominent intersections within Roman ruins is striking to even the casual visitor, there was often much more to them than a display of water:

> Way stations were for pausing, for lingering, for gathering informally, stopping-off places along a town's central circuit. Some, particularly those backed by benches or walls, were a species of small theater, their stages the busy streets and plazas alongside. Well placed for observing the human parade, with wide openings and angles of vision, they surely encouraged idling, though the provision of amenities answered practical needs too. Because most way stations tended to be restorative, they were not empty gestures but important servants of the urban symbiosis.[3]

These resting places were invariably out of the traffic while immediately adjacent to it, sheltered and less chaotic than the center of the markets, piazzas, or streets. They encouraged gathering, observation, and social discourse. Whenever one stepped into a Roman city—whether it be Massalia (Marseilles) in Gaul, Tipasa in Algeria, Gemila in Tunisia, Ephesus in Turkey, Pompeii and Ostia in Italy, or Rome itself—the generous furniture it offered in the form of benches, ledges, railings, colonnades, basin copings, and steps engendered an urban conviviality. These social and civic habits then became a characteristic of Roman culture, and a sign of its cohesion and unity.

In addition to these monumental and emblematic places to sit in ancient cities there were also, of course, less permanent arrangements made of wood: planks, benches, tables, and stalls, such as those that were heaped up and set on fire for Julius Caesar's funeral pyre by the rioting mob following his assassination. Plank benches and roughly made trestle tables were set up

---

3.   William L. MacDonald, *The Architecture of the Roman Empire, Vol. II: An Urban Appraisal*, Yale University Press, 1986, p. 105.

outdoors in the public realm seasonally, and this would remain true across Europe in the succeeding centuries. But with the end of the Roman Empire permanent public seating vanished, and streets and squares became less felicitous places to be: throughout the Middle Ages there was a marked absence of this civil ideal in seating.

Many prints of the late medieval and early Renaissance periods, including those by the Flemish master Pieter Bruegel the Elder, show figures—lords and ladies as well as peasants—seated upon the ground. Only occasionally are they shown seated upon wooden stools or rude chairs made from dowels and planks or rushes. The lack of outdoor furnishing in these images probably derives in part from the nature and uses of public space from classical antiquity to the late Renaissance. During these centuries, streets, plazas, and *fora* were places of movement, marketing and trading, religious and secular pageants, and displays of power and control, even executions. They were not designed for leisure and pleasure.

Urban spaces were also filled with work animals—horses, mules, donkeys, oxen—and various herds being brought to market: pigs, sheep, goats, cattle—along with carts and wagons of goods, carriages, pedestrians, and litters. There was a fair amount of mud and dust, mixed with manure, trash, and human excrement. The public realm was an active and messy place, neither intended nor particularly suitable for sitting about.

From early medieval times through much of the 14th century, most of the people represented in paintings, prints, and drawings are going about some sort of business. Those that are just hanging about or seated on some rock or lump of ancient ruin resemble what today we call the homeless, or vagrants. Convivial public seating for such social outcasts clearly wasn't encouraged.

(Today, the squares and souks within the Medina of Marrakech in Morocco and the regional trading centers in the mountains of western China or northern Vietnam still possess this jumble of people, animals, and goods, in the midst of which only rudimentary and makeshift seating is available—if there is any at all. People in public spaces in the developing world do, indeed, sit, but they do so either directly upon the pavement or on steps, a box, a bale of goods, or a plank bench.)

The same lack of seating existed within private parks and gardens; guests and travelers visited them regularly for centuries, and yet—aside from the delightful medieval invention of peculiar sofa-like arrangements fashioned of turf, which might truly be called "landscape" seats—one rarely sees the sort of furnishing that became common after the 16th century. When one examines prints, drawings, and paintings of European gardens through the Middle Ages, the historic figures, patrons, and guests represented therein are often riding or strolling. When they sit in full view—whether upright on a rock or sprawling about in their silks, taffetas, brocades, and furs—they are reposing on the ground.

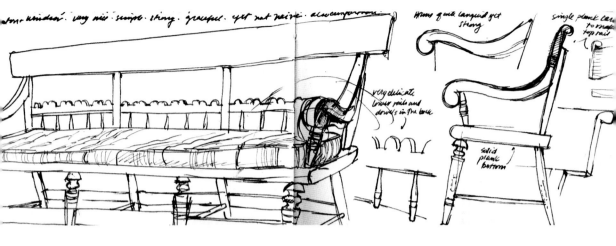

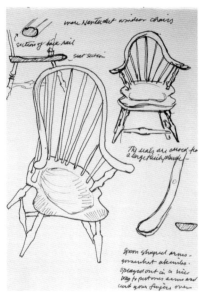

TOP A mid-19th-century country bench from central Pennsylvania. Almost all benches are really just stretched chairs. This one is a handsome combination of lathe-turned dowels, sawn planks—each of which has been worked with band saws and table saws to produce the two different curved molding profiles—along with solid carved arms. The balance between lines, planes, masses, and voids is remarkable. However, given the unforgiving plank seat, a cushion or pad is absolutely necessary, if one is to sit for any period of time. SB 120, pen and ink, 1999

BOTTOM Three different versions of the Windsor chair found on Nantucket. The left-hand sketch of one made by Frederick Slade between 1778 and 1800 has diagonal braces because the dowels of the back have been reduced to such thinness as to threaten their functionality. All have heavy carved plank seats. Note the wide spatulate (spoon shaped) arms on the right pair, which are remarkably comfortable and irresistibly cause one to take hold of their ends with one's fingers. SB 160, pen and ink, 2014

34 Chairs in my first apartment in Philadelphia after returning from living in Europe in 1974: a petite Viennese bentwood café chair by one of Thonet's competitors and two early 20th-century American wicker porch chairs. sb 35, pen and ink, 1976

2211 Locust — Bruce 76

LAURIE OLIN

TOP Furniture in the Villino at the American Academy in Rome: the first two items are small bedroom chairs, one peculiarly low to the floor, albeit extremely comfortable in a slouchy sort of way and probably intended for a child or a diminutive elderly person (a nonna or nonno); the larger armchair and sofa were covered in white linen canvas and equally comfortable. The fountain is in the Piazza of Santa Maria in Trastevere, which sits on a wedding cake of steps frequently seating many people. SB 147, Pen and ink, 2008

BOTTOM These drawings are of two of the most comfortable armchairs ever. They are English country house pieces from the turn of the 19th/20th century, but were encountered in an old mill that had been converted for summer guests at Ribas in Provence. Their soft slouchy shape, cool linen fabric, and long arms and seats were delightful in the stone building and heat of summer. SB 83, pen and ink, watercolor, 1991

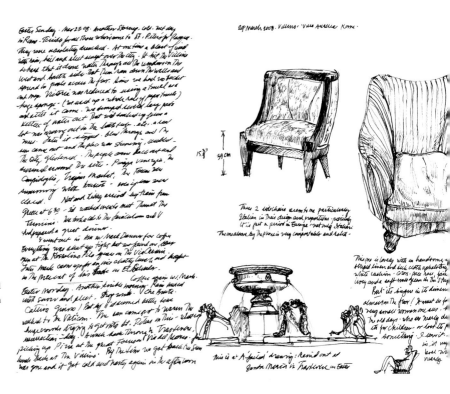

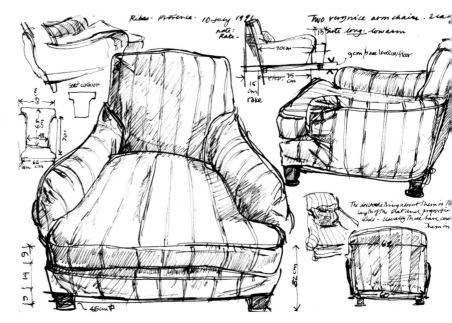

There is a pair of these to complement the huge sofa.

one of a set of 3 nesting side tables down in the Villino

They remind me of the small Viennese table at home in Phila.

These items of furniture are extremely comfortable, well proportioned and well made. They have white linen (cotton?) covering that is relatively heavy duty. They are elegant and cool in summer.

The sofa is nice and long. Nat slept in this one with room to spare. The length of the seat and its height seemed particularly good. They remind me of furnishings in English country houses as well as being associated with the Academy here and Il salone etc.

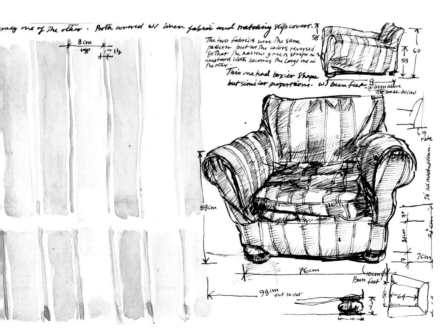

only one of the other. Both covered w/ linen fabric and matching slip covers.

The two fabrics were the same pattern but w/ the colors reversed so that the narrow green stripe in mustard cloth becomes the large one in the other.

This one had boxier shape but similar proportions — w/ bun feet armature the base below

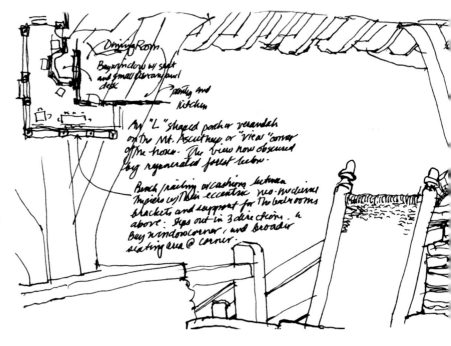

38

TOP This veranda in Cornish, New Hampshire, exudes sociability. Like many Victorian structures in New England, it combines rustic and urbane qualities. The parapet of the L-shaped porch, a deep-bracketed affair, has been developed as a continuous series of stone seat-walls with wood rail backs. To this have been added generous wicker chairs, rockers, and settees—an example of combining loose and fixed, hard and soft items to facilitate all manner of parties, events, quiet moments, and family retreats. SB 135, pen and ink, 2004

BOTTOM Sketch studies of bench and banquette seating designed by Charles Adams Platt for himself and friends in Cornish, New Hampshire, as part of his Americanized, country-villa vernacular. Whether working indoors or out, his furnishings are often generous as well as eccentric in their expression. These examples are both comfortable and convivial places to sit. SB 135, pen and ink, 2004

The Proud Verandah at "Crossways" Cornish Colony. N.H. 22 Aug 04
where we breakfasted on Max   good   Lanterns for
    Blumberg, Eduardo, Witold, VD+   candles to set out on
        Misty R., Lynn Sommers.   piers in evening.

The Bay
w/window
seat for
Reading.

...vortices - nooks - benches - portes. These... summer houses!

→ v. deep
4 ¾ length of this
sketchbook

Section of
small seat.

LAURIE OLIN

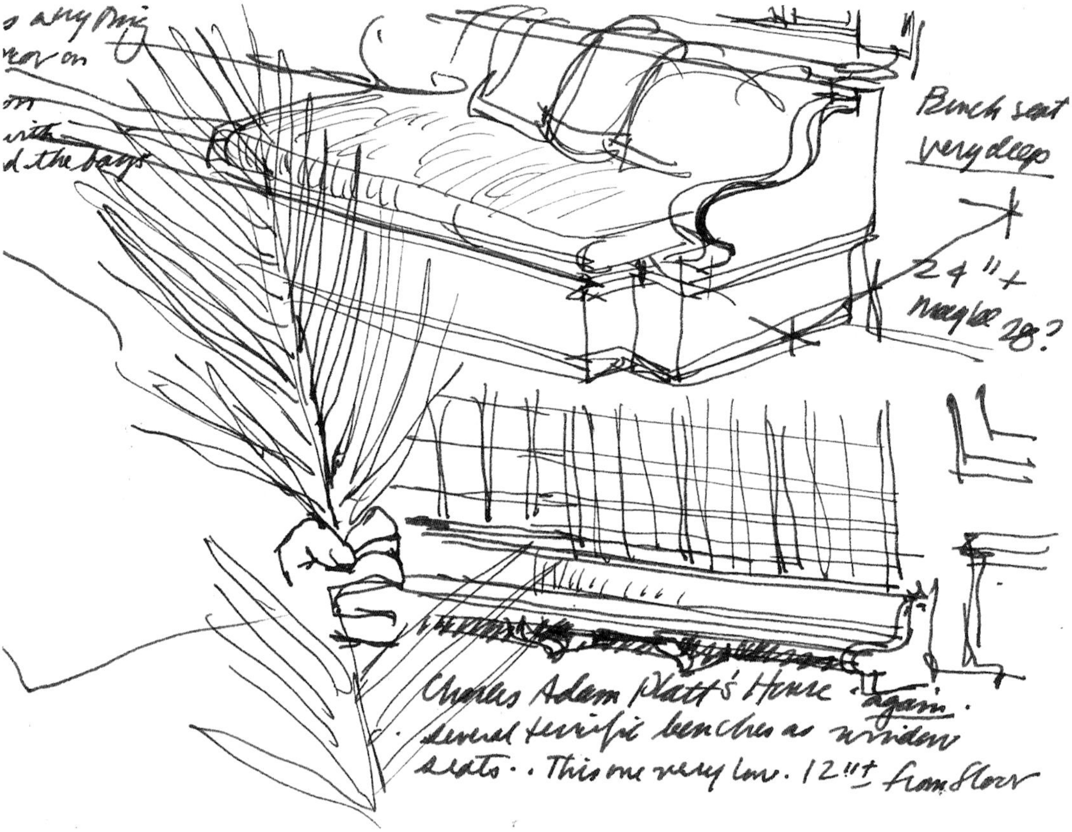

s any prin
rror on
om
ith
d the bags

Bench seat
very deep

24"+
maybe 28.?

Charles Adam Platt's House . again .
several terrific benches as window
seats . . This one very low. 12"+ from floor

Another bench of Platt's stretched along the portico of his house, made
with a deep seat, generous proportions, and a neoclassical touch as he
translates a bracket scroll into a chunky arm. sb 135, pen and ink, 2004

As changes in the economy, social order, art, and architecture transformed northern Italy in the mid-15th century, instances of seating in public
places began to reappear. Fernand Braudel and others have described the
emergence of personal space as one of the attendant phenomena of the
dismantling of the feudal system and the rise of merchant-based economies.[4]
With this came other changes: cities and dwellings once made from organic
and perishable materials were reconstructed in stone and brick; individual
chairs were introduced for indoor seating, and became increasingly popular;
and all manner of household furnishings, such as carpets and forks, were
invented and disseminated. The return of public seating was another aspect
of this remarkable cultural and material efflorescence.

One of the first instances of public seating was built into Florence's
Piazza Signoria, which by the beginning of the 1400s was framed by
generous stone benches on three sides. This piazza was at the heart of the
city and contained its principal municipal building. In addition to providing
bleachers for crowds during public ceremonies—the promulgation of
government edicts, funerals, wedding celebrations of dignitaries, religious
festivals, executions, investitures—these benches also offered a location
for casual meeting, discourse, and conversation related to civic and private
affairs; people of different classes sorted themselves out by rank on the
three tiers. Several of the benches were also covered for protection from sun
and rain. As Yvonne Elet has commented, this seating in the piazza facing
the Palazzo Vecchio "was emblematic of an open relationship between
government and public" and was "no doubt intended to project an image of
the regime as open, benevolent, and secure in its authority."[5]

Before long, several of the powerful families in Florence had incorporated
the notion of public seating in their own self-aggrandizing construction
projects. By the next century, the urban palaces of the Medici, Strozzi, and
Rucellai all had continuous, built-in stone benches flanking their entries and
running the entire length of their principal facades.[6] This was accomplished
through the metamorphosis of an architectural element known as "the water
table" that Florentine architects had adopted from their study of classical
ruins and the texts of Vitruvius. A continuous stone base found on traditional
Roman buildings, the water table functioned as a sort of splashguard to
protect the plaster of the upper wall from staining and erosion. By adding
a horizontal ledge to this hefty ribbon of stone, which the wall appeared

4.   Fernand Braudel, *Capitalism and Material Life: 1400–1800,* trans. Miriam Kochan, Littlehampton
Book Services Ltd., 1973, p. 65.
5.   Yvonne Elet, "Seats of Power: The Outdoor Benches of Early Modern Florence," *Journal of the
Society of Architectural Historians*, Vol. 61, No. 4 (Dec. 2002), p. 448. Elet offers an excellent account of
the public seating in northern Italy of the period.
6.   Elet, Ibid., pp. 447–459.

Ribas. Provence. July 8.9.91

The Chinoise bedroom in the mill

These wicker chairs (with and without arms), cushions, and wooden rush-bottom chair are clearly country furnishings—more of the sort one expects on a veranda than indoors in a bedroom, where these in fact were encountered in Provence. However, they seemed quite at home with the Chinese screen and rough stone walls. SB 83, pen and ink, 1991

LAURIE OLIN

Villa Tugendat, Brno
11 Mar

Entry from the road above.
What a truly beautiful and extraordinary structure.

X Hales   Lehmbrook
Sculpture –

The living space of Mies van der Rohe's Villa Tugendhat in Brno, Czech
Republic, with three of his revolutionary tubular metal frame chairs. SB
150, pen and ink, 2009

to sit upon, the water table offered a new function: seating for petitioners and others waiting for an audience with the noble inhabitants within. These benches would have served also as a gathering place for the family's allies and supporters—often armed gangs in the pay of the building's owner—or for casual encounters and observing the life of the street.

Although the benches installed by Cosimo de' Medici at the Pitti Palace may well have been the first to be created by a private citizen, by doing so he was deliberately echoing the benches at the Piazza della Signoria on the other side of the Arno and the civic authority they symbolically suggested. Seating built into the base of private palaces could also be seen, therefore, as a public gift to the citizens from the family within as well as a demonstration of *noblesse oblige* to be noted by their social peers and rivals. And when Florentine artists and architects migrated south to Rome, they carried this concept with them. Donato Bramante included a correspondingly generous seat at the base of the design for one of his most iconic works: the Tempietto at San Pietro in Montorio in Rome.

When I first encountered Santa Maria della Consolazione in Todi, in 1973, I was immediately struck by its affordance of sociability and I made a sketch of it, not realizing its innovative pedigree. Such seats also appeared in some of the most advanced, even radically modern works of the era, such as the Palazzo Farnese in Rome, which was begun by one of Bramante's assistants, Antonio Sangallo the Younger, and the Piccolomini Palazzo in Pienza by Bernardo Rossellino, where there are generous and continuous benches on three sides of its famous town square—one facing the principal street, the others the intimate Piazza del Duomo. These benches are accompanied by a footrest, a feature that elevates them slightly from the piazza, conferring both separation and a degree of privileged status—along with the added benefit of keeping one's feet and clothing out of whatever water and refuse might be on the pavement below.

This feature was present at a number of other later *palazzi* benches of the same period in Florence, Urbino, and Rome, many of which are still well used today. I've sat on the benches in Pienza as well as those at the Palazzo Farnese in Rome on several occasions, happily surveying and sketching the passing crowd and urban scene. Integrated as they are into the masonry fabric of the structures, the benches also form a level base for the façade for these important monumental buildings, which in turn shape the public spaces they front onto.

There doesn't appear to have been much further development of public seating in urban spaces until the mid-17th century, when there was an outburst of building in Rome that included the creation of numerous fountains. One of their frequent and fundamental design features was the fabrication of generous stone copings, many of which are a comfortable height to lean or sit upon. In prior centuries, paintings often depicted saints, mythological figures, and members of the nobility within gardens or cloisters seated upon the rims of pools and fountains. Now the man in the street could do so as well. Gian Lorenzo Bernini's studio produced a number of what are arguably among the greatest fountains in Western history, which happen to possess attractive and sittable copings.

The sketches and study models that survive from Bernini's hand and studio also suggest that the sculptor often conceived of enclosing these basins with stone bollards connected by wrought-iron railings. Mostly this was to keep horses at bay, and carriages from colliding with the fountains themselves, but on occasion they were also designed to function as de facto benches. These urban amenities—covered loggias, stone copings and benches, baroque fountains—became not only hallmarks of the Italian Renaissance but also iconic symbols of public space.

Not surprisingly, some of the earliest depictions of non-monumental outdoor furnishing occur in the Netherlands, at the time when notions of material comfort, personal freedom, and communal self-governance were burgeoning. One of the only landscape paintings made by Vermeer (c. 1659), now in the Rijksmuseum, is of a house front and small pedestrian lane in Delft. It also depicts a pair of stone benches set into the masonry on either side of a residential entry door and supplemented by a small plank seat placed at 90 degrees to the others. Clearly intended for the owners and servants of the house to use, whether simply for sitting in the fresh air to perform household tasks (sewing, shelling peas, etc.) or for socializing, gossiping, and watching passersby. This appearance of outdoor seating points to changing attitudes toward public space—whether it be the street, the canal, or the square. It is the beginning of urban middle-class outdoor accommodation.

In the 1500s and 1600s, a new form of seating began to appear in parks and gardens as well, in judiciously placed small pavilions and temples. Commonly referred to as "seats" and designed to offer shelter from the sun and rain (as well as a measure of privacy from gardeners and workmen), these creations would often look out on a pleasing prospect and contain one or more generous benches.

Because gardens and parks remained exclusively private well into the 18th century, there was no call for "public" seating. There were litters and sedan chairs, of course, and servants were often pressed into carrying folding stools and other furnishings out onto terraces and into gardens for both ordinary use and special occasions. Still, depictions of people in gardens and parks show them continuing to lie about on the turf, frequently on capes, shawls, or blankets. Several delightful Elizabethan and Jacobean miniatures depict poets and courtiers lying about recalling the words and green thoughts of Andrew Marvell, with no bench or furniture in sight.

(Despite my interest and curiosity regarding landscape furniture, I must confess that there is an undeniably luxurious aspect to lying directly on the

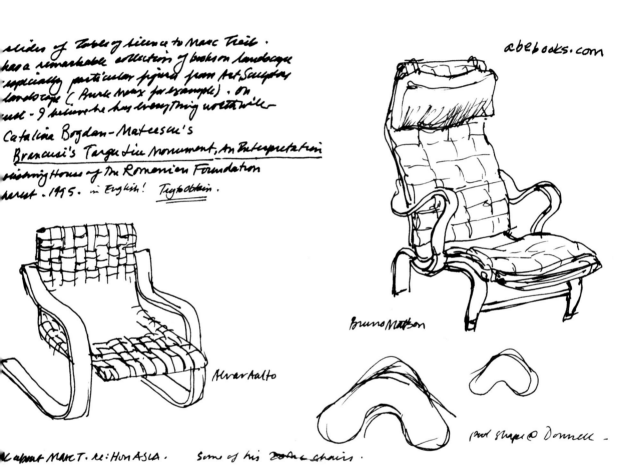

slides of Tables of science to Marc Treib.
has a remarkable collection of books on landscape
especially particular figures from Art Sculptors
landscape (Burle Marx for example) . on
use - I believe he has everything worthwhile
Catalina Bogdan-Mateescu's
Brancusi's Targue Jiu Monument, An Interpretation
visiting House of the Romanian Foundation
bucurest . 1995 . in English! Try to obtain .

abebooks.com

Bruno Mattson

Alvar Aalto

pad shape @ Donnell -

к about MARC T. re: Hon ASLA .   Some of his Zofac chairs .

Two chairs by modern masters that were early examples of bending and
folding plywood to make continuous structures that could encompass
support for the seat, arms, and backs. These are by Alvar Aalto and
Bruno Mathsson, both of whom worked closely with the timber
industry and fabricators in Scandinavia. Like the furniture of Charles
and Ray Eames in America, which similarly explored the possibilities of
glue lamination (plywood), bending, folding, and machine presses, their
work has a warm, sensuous character that has become associated with
classic or mid-century modernism. sb 133, pen and ink, 2002

LAURIE OLIN

Feby, 2002. Reflections in situation at Tirgu-Jiu. Romania.

How to destroy a work of art
← This is how Brancusi's stools on the Avenue of
looked before the obsessive planting and fami
the communist landscape architects in the
Tirgu-Jiu — as seen in an old photograph
clear and simple. ...

Hand-carved stone stools line The Avenue of the Heroes as part of the sculpture ensemble created by Constantin Brancusi in 1937 in Târgu Jiu, Romania. One of the first true abstract sculptors, Brancusi ritualized the act of sitting by transforming humble folk elements as part of his monumental memorial in a sequence of civic spaces. SB 129, pen and ink, 2002

earth in lush grasses, especially in the sun, as many a well-fed picnicker who has fallen asleep in these circumstances will agree. One of the more evocative depictions of this is a painting at the Metropolitan Museum of Art by Pieter Bruegel known as *The Harvesters*, which depicts a farmer lying asleep in a wheat field with his scythe after lunch.)

Benches designed specifically for parks and gardens first seem to appear at the beginning of the 18th century. The designer in particular who brought an interest and knowledge of interior furnishing out into these spaces was William Kent—perhaps the most important innovator in the development of the English Landscape Garden during this period. Kent began his career as a painter and interior designer, apprenticing for a number of years in Rome, where he absorbed an enormous amount regarding the art and design of the day.[7] As a result he became a favorite guide for wealthy English lords and tourists, thereby visiting villas, palaces, gardens, and parks throughout Italy and soaking up a wealth of design ideas, motifs, and methods. After returning to England, Kent designed some of the most sumptuous interiors in the history of European architecture, including their furniture.

As a designer of gardens and landscapes, Kent created seating for a number of pavilions and follies. A contemporary of Giambattista Piranesi and Nicholas Hawksmoor, whose work he clearly knew, Kent was unusually versatile; his designs range from wildly exuberant and over-scaled to delicate and elegant, even austere. In part due to the relatively mild climate, much of his park furniture was made of wood and remained permanently out of doors, albeit usually sheltered in small kiosks, pavilions, or more elaborate temples and follies, such as that for the Praeneste at Rousham in Oxfordshire or Merlin's Cave in Kensington Gardens.

In her monumental work, *Keywords in American Landscape Design*, Therese O'Malley offers a lengthy section on garden "seats."[8] Many of the examples she gives from the late Colonial and Federal periods were derived largely from designs published in England by Kent's immediate predecessors and contemporaries: Batty Langley, William Chambers, and James Gibbs. O'Malley points out that later writers and theorists such as Isaac Ware and Humphry Repton "focused upon seats as places of rest, terminations of walks, or vantage points from which to contemplate views," and that this

---

7.   One of the most recent documents regarding Kent's career is *William Kent: Designing Georgian Britain*, Ed. Susan Weber, Victoria and Albert Museum Exhibition Catalogue, Yale University Press, 2013; see Susan Weber, "The Well of Inspiration: Sources for Kent's Furniture Designs," pp. 449-467, and Susan Weber, "Kent and Georgian Baroque Style in Furniture: Domestic Commissions," pp. 469-525. Earlier standard biographies of Kent include those by Margaret Jourdain and Michael Wilson. There is also a catalogue of his drawings and garden career by John Dixon Hunt.

8.   Therese O'Malley, *Keywords in American Landscape Design*, Yale University Press, 2010. Numerous pavilions referred to as garden seats or follies by Kent are illustrated in John Harris, "Garden Buildings," pp. 393-411, in *William Kent: Designing Georgian Britain*, op. cit.

was related to a traditional concept whereby the preferred route through a garden was punctuated by stops to enjoy panoramas, or scenes rich with allusion, and for rest, contemplation, or conversation. These seats weren't located just anywhere in parks and gardens; they were integral parts of larger compositions, and used as devices to help organize and regulate them.

But it wasn't until the jardin anglais became fashionable in France and Italy in the latter part of the 18th century that—in addition to its curvilinear walks and ponds, groves, greensward, and exotic pavilions—the now-ubiquitous wooden bench was introduced. For the Petit Trianon at Versailles, Marie Antoinette's designers produced wooden benches in three distinct styles for different parts of the garden. The most refined of these, which had elegant tracery and sculpted backs, were placed adjacent to the Pavilion; the heftier, neoclassical ones, with turned legs and balusters supporting the back rail, were scattered along paths and among the flower beds; and the even simpler, more rustic ones were for the distant, wilder areas. One of the results of the research undertaken during the restoration of Versailles after a devastating hurricane in 1999 was that these benches were rediscovered and recreated. Subsequently a company, Jardins du Roi Soleil, has been set up to reproduce and market reproductions of them, along with other furnishings from the palace.[9]

A notable feature of several of the prominent Jardins Anglais designed in late 18th-century France was that of paths leading through diverse settings containing evocative architecture and landscape tableaux. This emphasis on variety called for additional types of seating appropriate to the mood and character of each location: moss-covered benches, stone seats, and rustic efforts made with tree branches and twigs. Several prominent examples were situated in the bucolic park of Ermenonville designed by the Marquis de Girardin to honor Jean-Jacques Rousseau. To prompt the appropriate reveries in the visitor, some seats look out to the island planted with poplars that houses the philosopher's tomb; another is just beside the door of his rustic cottage.[10] Michael Jakob describes these seats, which are sometimes accompanied by nearby inscriptions, as a "machine a contemplar," particularly toward Rousseau's life and writing.

The transformation of public space that began in the 18th century and spilled over into the 19th played a part in evolving attitudes regarding community, nationality, and personal freedom. Most dramatically, many parks were thrown open to the public after the Revolution. One has only to look at prints of Camille Desmoulins haranguing the crowd in the garden of the Palais Royal, exhorting them to end the monarchy in France, or

---

9.   "Antennae," *The World of Interiors*, October 2014, pp. 44-47.
10.   Michael Jakob, *Poétique du Banc*, Éditions Macula, 2014 pp. 67-93; see prints pp. 67, 85, 89.

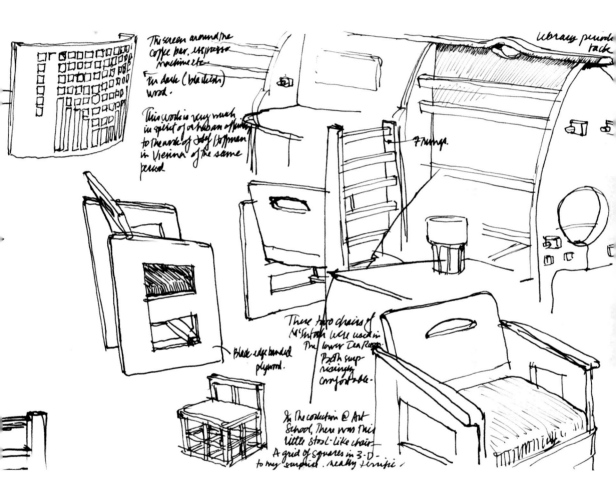

The handwritten notes in the sketch read:

This screen around the coffee bar, espresso machine etc.

In dark (blackish) wood.

This work is very much in spirit of urban art/furniture to the work of Josef Hoffmann in Vienna of the same period

library periodical rack

Fringe.

These two chairs of McIntosh were used in the lower Tea Room. Both surprisingly comfortable.

Black edge banded plywood.

In the collection @ Art School, there was this little stool-like chair. A grid of squares in 3-D – to my surprise, really terrific.

The desire to rethink and refresh the design of furniture was an interest of a number of architects in the 20th century, especially the early modernists. Charles Rennie Mackintosh designed these interesting pieces for the student canteen in his Glasgow School of Art, completed in 1909. SB 126, pen and ink, 2000

LAURIE OLIN

Painted wicker furniture in the loggia of the Villa at La Foce in Tuscany,
from which one surveys the garden and day; the perfect place to read,
converse with a friend, dine, or take a nap. sb 116, watercolor, 1998

subsequent views of crowds in the Tuileries following the Revolution to understand how important these spaces and their uses were in the forming of modern society. For such a turn of events to occur, it is also axiomatic that the crowds were able to do more than walk or stand about in these spaces. Now they could spend hour after hour there—reading, talking, debating, listening to, and watching each other—in no small part because they could simply *sit* there for extended periods of time.

By mid-century, French parks had become an integral part of bourgeois life and benches had become an integral part of parks; they frequently appear in painting and writing as props for commentary on social behavior. The strange 1857 Biedermeier novel of manners, *Der Nachsommer,* by Adalbert Stifter, is populated with benches of two sorts: those for communing with one's surroundings and those for communing with one's lover.[11] The first sort are scattered throughout the landscape and named according to their adjacent trees—cherry, ash, linden, etc. Offering free and sweeping views of the surroundings, they also attempt to exert an element of control, directing the strolling viewer where to stop and view a particular, proposed ideal world. The second sort provide men and women with an opportunity for flirting, courtship, and romance. In some of their most evocative and engaging works, Édouard Manet and Claude Monet depict such scenes with a calm familiarity, no doubt combining their devotion to presenting contemporary "real" life with what was by the late 1870s common social behavior.[12]

The newly constructed boulevards and parks of London, Berlin, Paris, New York, Barcelona, and elsewhere in the second half of the 19th century were made possible in part by the social and political revolutions of the era and in part by the generation of new wealth and tax revenue resulting from industrial expansion and the development of a consumer society. The streets and squares of these cities provided an arena where important visions of urban life and real estate development combined with contests for control by the state.

These new civic spaces were furnished extensively with mass-produced items that had been designed in the offices of park departments and landscape architects—most notably those of Adolphe Alphand's *Bureau des Ponts et Chaussées* in Paris and of Olmsted and Vaux in New York. Many of the men who worked in these offices had originally been trained as engineers, architects, or gardeners. Along with their development of drains, hydrants, lighting fixtures, tree grates, and waste bins, they developed a

---

11.   Michael Jakob, ibid, pp. 96-110.

12.   T. J. Clark in *The Painting and Modern Life* offers a lengthy discussion of the social behavior of the period utilizing paintings by Manet, Monet, and Renoir as examples.

variety of benches that utilized metal castings for structural support and arms, and repetitive wooden slats for seats and backs. The limited parts were both reproducible and interchangeable, making manufacture, shipping, assembly, installation, repair, and replacement easy and relatively inexpensive. Thus was born the familiar Central Park bench with its circular arms, the simple Parisian plank bench with its straight vertical back, and a third that recalls a rolltop desk with its undulating shape and small slats, all of which are still widely used.

While forerunners or prototypes may have existed for a time, one of the earliest recordings of these familiar Paris park benches occurs in the landmark publication *Les Promenades de Paris* by Alphand, published in sections between 1867 and 1873, which records the transformation of Paris, beginning with his appointment in 1853 as director of the park service and subsequently while he was Director of Public Works under Baron Haussmann's Prefecture of the Seine. This reference book contains not only views of the parks with technical details of their construction but also engravings of standardized furnishings and their deployment in over twenty public parks and forty miles of streets and boulevards.[13] Studying the dozens of park plans, one discovers that these simple two-meter-long benches were deployed in vast quantities—on the medians of new boulevards and almost continuously around the perimeter walkways of nearly every new square. In the brief period between 1853 and 1870, Alphand and his bureau created a version of civic space that defined the public realm, and much of it survives today, for others to maintain and build upon.

13.   Jean-Charles Adolphe Alphand, *Les Promenades de Paris*, J. Rothschild, Ed. 1867–73: a reduced-size facsimile has been published by Princeton Architectural Press, 1984. The plates of the original folios are unnumbered, but the straight plank bench appears on the plate entitled "Bois de Boulogne, Portes, Grilles, Bancs"; the curving one with multiple dowels and another plank and metal frame bench with a familiar pitched back appear on a plate for details of the "Square des Batignolles." A more elaborate metal bench with three planks—one for the back and one for a seat on either side—appears on a plate following the plans for a number of the squares titled simply "Voie Publique, Detail."

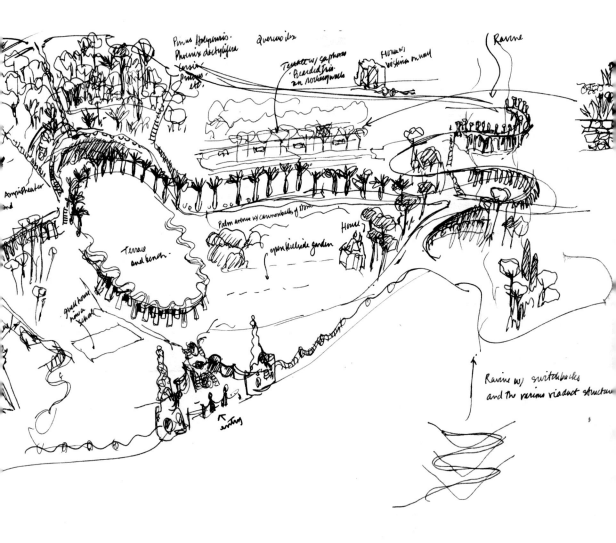

Among the most amazing of all seating that has been worked into its setting as both infrastructure and ornament may be that of Antoni Gaudí and Josep Maria Jujol's extravagant undulating ceramic-covered seat wall or bench, which has become an iconic image for Park Güell and the city of Barcelona. It not only provides both a parapet railing for a dramatic overlook of the city and ample seating for crowds that gather on the terrace but also offers a number of separate spaces for small groups and socializing. This seat wall grows out of a larger and ubiquitous geometry that invigorates the entire park—a fractal relationship of curvilinear regression. While affording the humble service of being merely a bench and eliminating clutter, it also serves as the "genius of the place." SB 81, pen and ink, 1991

LAURIE OLIN

Latace. 29 June 1998

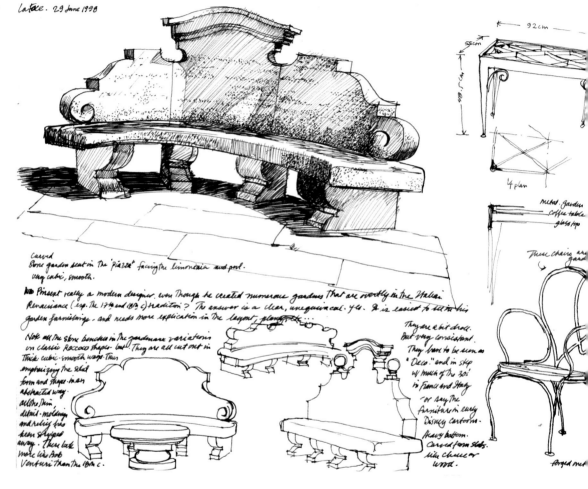

92cm

55cm

4 plan

metal garden
coffee table
glass top

These chairs are
garden

Carved
Stone garden seat in the "piazza" facing the limonaia and pool.
very cubic, smooth.

Was Pinsent really a modern designer, even though he created numerous gardens that are overtly in the Italian
Renaissance (esp. the 17th and 18th c.) tradition? The answer is a clear, unequivocal. Yes. It is easiest to see in his
garden furnishings - and needs more explication in the layout, plans...

Note all the stone benches in the gardens are variations
on classic Rococo shapes - but they are all cut out in
thick cubic-smooth ways. Thus
emphasizing the ideal
form and shapes in an
abstracted way.
All the trim,
detail, molding
and relief has
been stripped
away. These look
more like Bob
Venturi than the 18th c.

They are a bit droll.
But very consistent.
They have to be seen as
"Deco" and in step
w/ much of the 30's
in France and Italy
- or say the
furniture in early
Disney cartoons.
Heavy bottom.
Curved form slats.
like chaise or
wood.

forged me

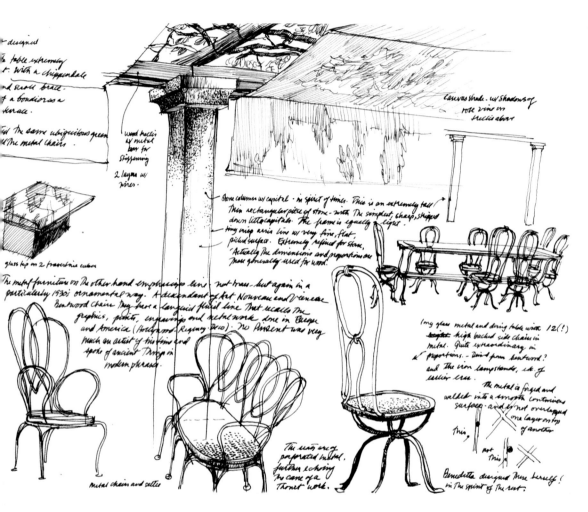

Garden furniture designed by Cecil Pinsent for Iris Origo's villa, La Foce,
in Tuscany, exhibits stylistic gestures associated with inter-war era Art
Deco, regardless of medium. These objects combine a stripped-down
neoclassicism, a playful touch, and a tendency to flatness and precise line.
SB 116, pen and ink, 1998

LAURIE OLIN

In addition to this supply of inexpensive and ubiquitous bench seating for the growing middle class to utilize, metal chairs suitable for outdoor use were also mass-produced and installed widely. These turn up in well-known paintings and photographs of the time—for example, in Manet's 1862 painting of the demi-monde in the Tuileries.[14] His depiction of the repetitive curving scrolls of the backs and frames supporting the dished metal seats of these familiar chairs is as clear-eyed and loving as that of the silks and taffetas worn by the women and top hats by the men. These chairs—one of which I photographed on my first trip to Europe—had only recently replaced the earlier wooden ones when Manet made this painting. They remained in use in Parisian parks until the 1940s, when they began to be displaced by those with metal frames and curved wooden slats, which in turn have been replaced more recently by several lighter models.[15]

The combination of fixed benches and loose chairs promulgated by the Parisian bureaucracy of the Second Empire has proved to be one of the most felicitous furnishing strategies for public space yet devised—so much so that it was taken up in private gardens. In more than a few of Claude Monet's paintings of Giverny, for example, one finds a curving, slatted bench with a relaxed backrest surrounded by moveable armchairs of wood and woven wicker.[16]

One development of the international proliferation of public parks in the latter third of the 19th century was the invention across the channel of the now familiar English park bench. This seemingly anonymous piece of outdoor furniture, made entirely of wood—once of oak, now usually of teak—exists in a variety of models marketed today under a number of regional and country place names (Mendip, Scarborough, York, etc.). One manufacturer claims to have made them since 1883. Others claim to have originated them using salvaged teak from the decks of naval vessels at the cessation of World War I. While this recycling is admirable, the origin of the style seems to be earlier.

Frederic Law Olmsted's vision for American cities was truly grand. He proposed the creation of not only parks but also parkways to link them in a carefully arranged configuration, often incorporating rivers, escarpments, marshes, shorelines, and derelict lands to provide greenways for the health and well being of all citizens. In light of all the sweeping landscape vistas

14.   The painting *Music in the Tuileries*, by Édouard Manet, is jointly owned by the National Gallery in London and the Hugh Lane Gallery in Dublin; in 2014 it was hanging in Dublin.
15.   The furniture most in use at the time of writing is made by the French manufacturer Fermob.
16.   Photographs of the furnishing of the Giverny garden appear in numerous books on Claude Monet; examples include: *Monet's Years at Giverny: Beyond Impressionism*, the Metropolitan Museum of Art, Abrams, 1978, and Claire Joyes, *Monet at Giverny*, Mayflower Books, 1975.

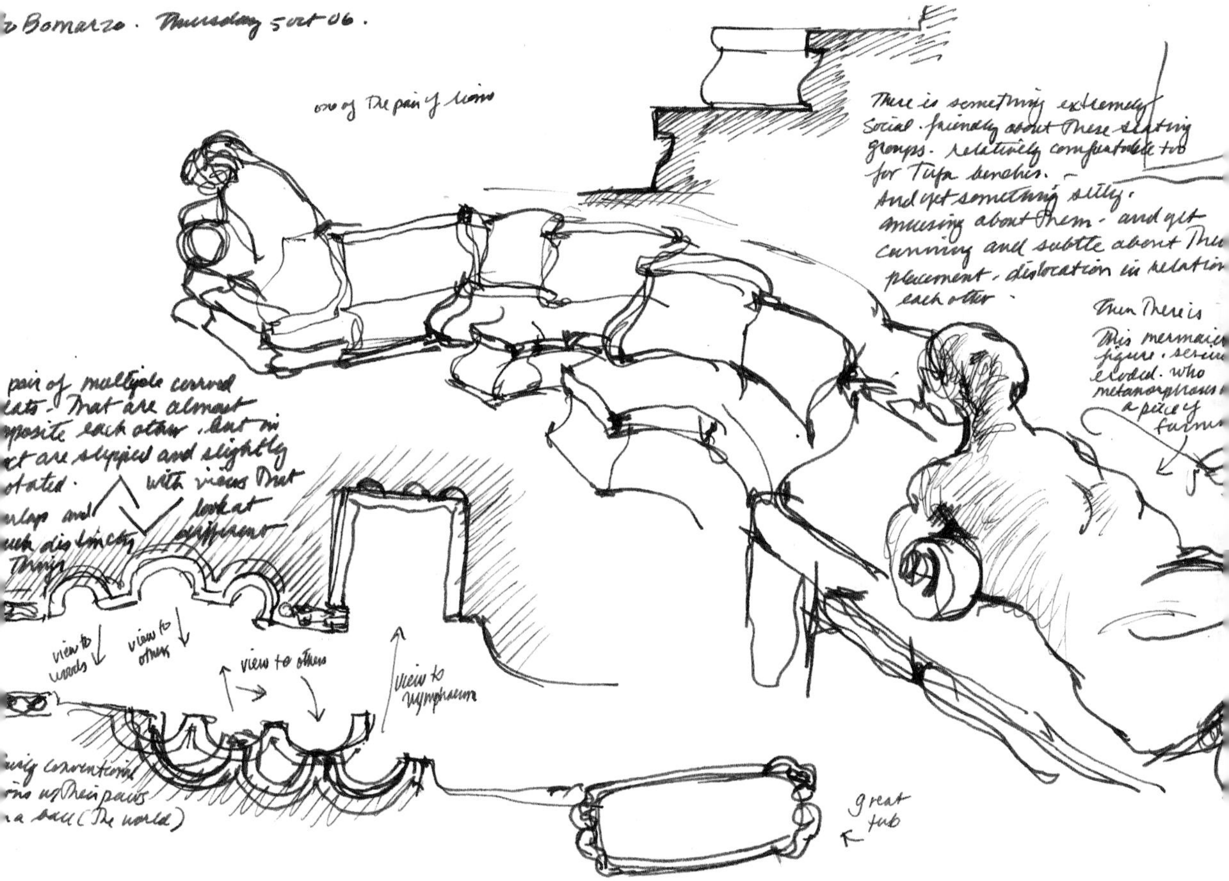

Bomarzo. Thursday 5 oct 06.

one of the pair of lions

There is something extremely
social, friendly about these seating
groups. relatively comfortable too
for Tufa benches.
And yet something silly.
amusing about them. and yet
cunning and subtle about their
placement. dislocation in relation
each other.

Then there is
this mermaid
figure. serene
eroded. who
metamorphoses
a piece of
furn...

pair of multiple curved
seats. that are almost
opposite each other. but in
fact are slightly and slightly
rotated. with views that
overlap and look at
each distinctly different
thing.

view to woods ↓   view to others ↓   → view to others ↓   view to nymphaeum

very conventional
ones up their pairs
a seat (the world)

great tub ←

More fantasia; stone benches carved into rock outcrops. Here is design
achieved by a combination of subtraction (carving) and addition in
bizarre fashion, forming integral seating groups at Bomarzo, Italy. SB
144, pen and ink, 2006

LAURIE OLIN

that he and his colleagues managed to conjure into reality—including their embodiment of the aesthetic of the picturesque in Central Park and the sublime in portions of Prospect Park—and the spectacular rocks and cataracts of Yosemite and Niagara Falls that he endeavored to protect, the mundane topic of seating and benches may seem beneath consideration and of little consequence. In fact, however, the Olmsted office devoted considerable attention and effort throughout its history to a multiplicity of seating designs. For all the grand visions and artistic mastery of landscape form, it was on these benches within their compositions that much of people's experience of the parks actually took place.

For example, continuous, comfortable wooden benches line the length of both sides of a tunnel leading into the long meadow of Prospect Park, providing ample opportunity for dozens of people to sit in the shade with a light breeze in the worst of the hot days of New York in the summer. These unusually long and generous benches allowed individuals to sit far enough apart for comfort but close enough to be friendly or curious about each other without impingement, all the while able to observe those walking by as they entered or left the park—greeting friends, studying strangers, checking out their fashions and manner. In one Olmsted park after another there are pavilions, music groves, and terraces, all of which had built-in seating. On the United States Capitol grounds in Washington, DC, there is an artificial grotto with multiple drinking water taps for overheated visitors that also incorporates a number of built-in stone banquettes for the weary.

Comparable to the productions of Alphand in Paris, one sees in the many built projects of Olmsted and Vaux an exploitation of industrial methods and assembly in the manufacture and installation of vast quantities of seating. They skillfully employed cast-iron and precut standardized parts along with stencils and templates to shape repetitive units, initiating the mass-production of items whose imagery was inspired by classical ornament and the machine age—in effect, a Ruskinian industrial aesthetic. Ready examples of this can be seen not only in historic photos of Central Park but also in the continuous belts of restored iron and wood benches on The Mall leading to Bethesda Fountain.

There was a significant difference between the office of Olmsted and Vaux in New York and that of Alphand in Paris. Whereas the French bureau and its engineers purposely produced a limited number of standard prototypes for public seating that could be produced in mass quantity quickly, Olmsted's stable of architects and draftsmen produced almost endless inventions and variations in park furnishings, among which were innumerable benches. In addition to twenty bridges and overpasses that are all different from one another, the familiar so-called "Central Park bench" was in fact only one of many developed for that park—not to mention an array of others that were deployed elsewhere.

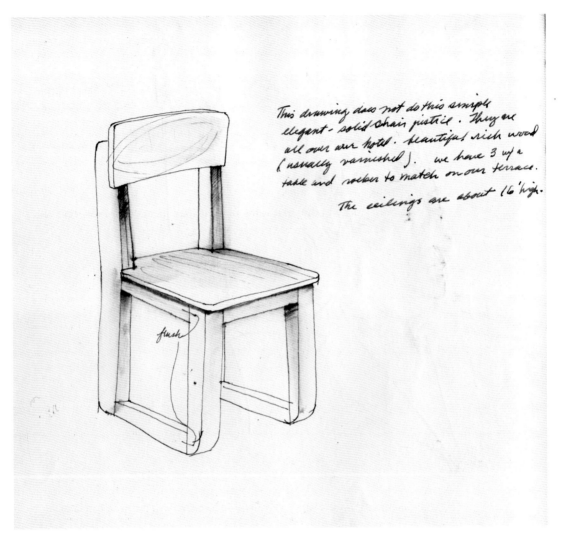

This drawing does not do this simple elegant - solid chair justice. They are all over our hotel. beautiful rich wood (usually varnished). we have 3 w/a table and rocker to match on our terrace.

The ceilings are about 16' high.

flush

This handsome and very solid wood café chair was one of a group in a hotel courtyard in Mazatlán. There is an elegant simplicity to it that one finds often in the countryside—not only in Mexico but in many countries. SB 19, pen and ink, 1968

LAURIE OLIN

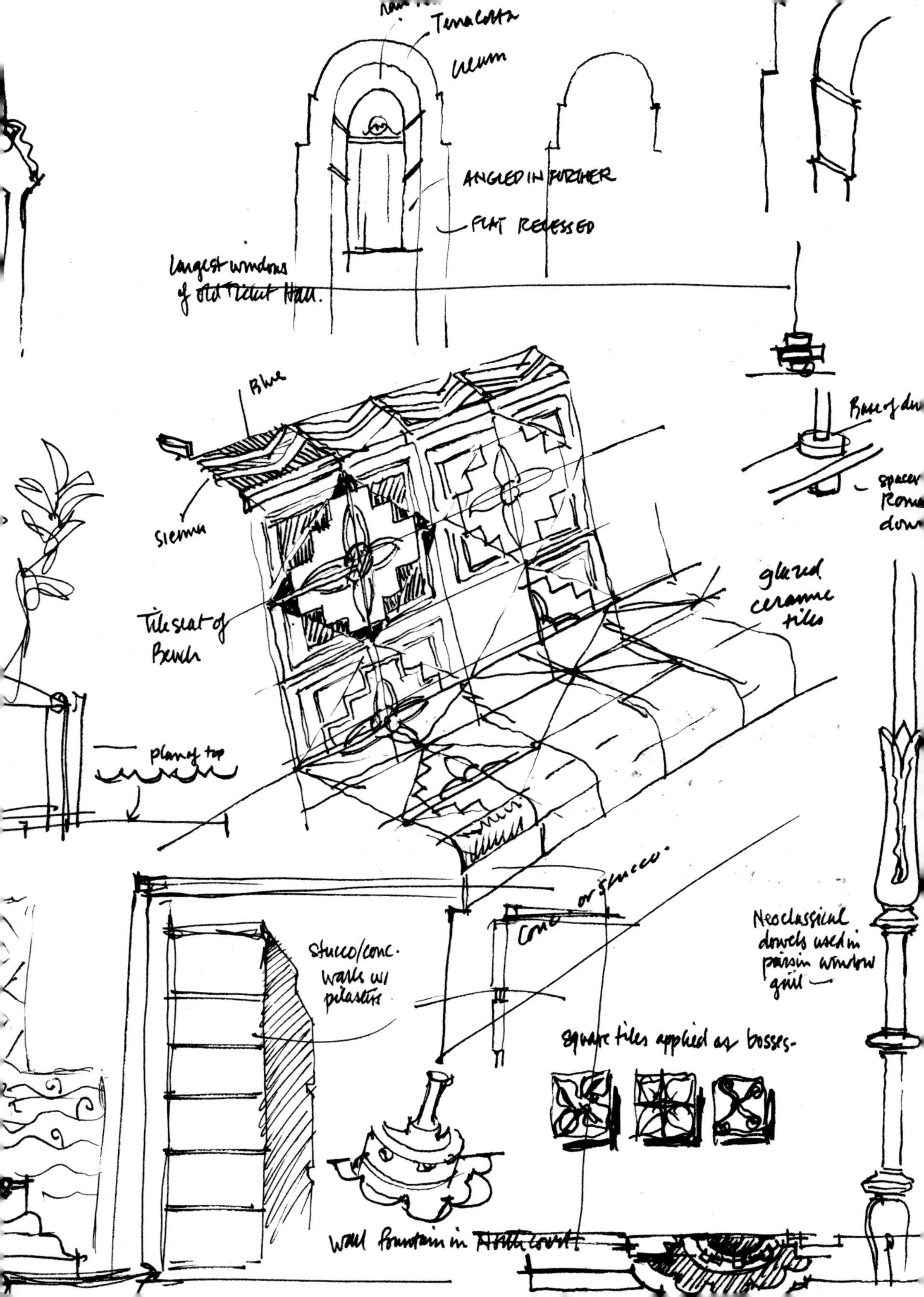

Terracotta
cream

ANGLED IN FURTHER

FLAT RECESSED

Largest windows
of old Ticket Hall.

Base of d...

spacer
Roma...
dow...

Blue

sienna

glazed
ceramic
tiles

Tile seat of
Bench

plank top

Stucco/conc.
walls w/
pilasters

cove or stucco.

Neoclassical
dowels used in
passin window
grill

square tiles applied as bosses.

Wall fountain in Hobb court

64

Athens - 29 May 1980. Drinking wine at cafe near Roman Agora. Dogs asleep in the street, cars
The city is completely overrun with European and American tourists. The Scandinavian and germans outnumber
waiters fighting over customers and turf - 'where to stand' etc..

PREVIOUS SPREAD Another example of public seating integral to the base of a building can be seen at the Spanish-revival Union Station in Los Angeles, where colorful tiles are draped like blankets onto several concrete benches built into window recesses facing a small public garden. SB 80, pen and ink, 1990

ABOVE Simple, sturdy wooden chairs spill out of a café and across a quiet lane near the Agora in Athens, Greece. SB 39, pen and ink, 1980

LAURIE OLIN

Calvert Vaux, Jacob Wrey Mould, and Frederick Clarke Withers were principal designers during this period in the Olmsted office; all English architects, they had been heavily influenced by Owen Jones, whose publication *Grammar of Ornament* had a marked impact on late-Victorian architecture. Oriental, Romanesque, medieval, Gothic, and neoclassical motifs were combined with the employment of mechanized processes to manufacture a diversity of site features and furniture in combinations of wood, metal, and stone. They also shared a predilection for floral motifs associated with transcendental and romantic attitudes. Like William Morris and others in England, these men wanted to create an environment of quality and amenity while using machine-tool processes to introduce art and educated taste to the public and working people.[17]

In the latter part of the 19th century, both Europe and America were industrializing at a rapid rate. As railroad engines rolled off production lines in Philadelphia, Birmingham, and Manchester, and steel rails were being laid across continents, as steel frame buildings with passenger elevators were being erected, along with elaborate metal-and-glass shopping arcades from Cleveland and Chicago to Paris and London, urban sophisticates developed a nostalgia for Europe's agrarian past and America's rapidly vanishing wilderness.

As a result, an alternative convention to this pervasive machine-tool aesthetic began emerging in parks and gardens on both sides of the Atlantic—often within the same offices that were producing the industrialized furnishings. This outburst of design and construction encompassed a mélange of rustic pavilions, railings, benches, chairs, and footbridges that offered (manufactured, really) an image of rural simplicity and life in the wilderness and on the frontier. What might be described as something of a Daniel Boone–baroque or Paul Bunyan–rococo style of bark, thatch, and twisting branches appeared in parks in Paris, Philadelphia, and New York, as well as on the grounds of châteaux and villas throughout Europe.

In sharp contrast to the pared down, almost nautical classicism of replicable cast-iron features, this faux-rustic furnishing trend went so far as to employ reinforced ferro-cement techniques that had only recently been developed in architecture and engineering to construct fake log bridges and

17.   Among the many dozens of publications in recent decades regarding the practice of Olmsted and Vaux, one of the only ones that clearly presents illustrations of this aspect of the work is Bruce Kelly, Gail Travis Guillet and Mary Ellen Hern's *Art of the Olmsted Landscape*, published by the New York Landmarks Preservation Commission in 1981, pp. 35, 36, 38, 42, 47, 57, 80–82. This book served as the catalogue of a major exhibition of photographs, prints, and drawings at the Metropolitan Museum of Art in New York City that same year.

27 July 68 - anne in the Seminole chair.

A rustic version of an Adirondack chair in the original manner at a
summer cabin, Amagansett, New York. SB 18, graphite pencil on coated
paper, 1968

LAURIE OLIN

stairways, overlooks and gazebos. Examples of this style can still be found in diverse parts of the United States.[18]

One variation of this occurred in the furnishings created for the United States National Parks and their rugged landscapes. Thirteen years after the National Park Service was founded, the stock market crash of 1929 ushered in the Great Depression. From 1933 to 1941 the FDR administration undertook a major effort to put Americans to work, part of which involved the construction of roads, trails, bridges, shelters, and lodges in parks across the country. The resulting infrastructure and architectural elements frequently employed mythologizing imagery that consciously evoked a frontier ethos of rough-hewn logs and hefty masonry. Many benches in this neo-pioneer mode can still be found along trails and around campgrounds and visitor centers of the National Park System.

Serviceable as seats and enduring through seasons of rough weather and hard use, they have become—like Smokey the Bear—a venerable symbol of the Park Service and evoke a nostalgic era of America: a bit awkward but well meaning and straightforward, like the cowboys portrayed by Gary Cooper and John Wayne a decade later. Even so, such logs and Adirondack twiggery that may make acceptable benches in the High Sierras or Appalachians were no longer favored by urban designers and landscape architects after World War II.

Many of the well-known American landscape architects of the first half of the twentieth century—Warren Manning, Ellen Biddle Shipman, Fletcher Steele—had little interest in thinking about seating within the public and private spaces they created. One of the rare exceptions to this was Beatrix Jones Farrand, little of whose work survives. A garden that does, however, which happens to be one of her two great masterpieces, Dumbarton Oaks in Washington, DC, is chock-a-block with places to sit.[19] One bench and seat after another is located in a particular place in the garden (at the end of a walk, in a corner, at the top of a stair) with a different aspect, and made in a fresh manner with a variety of materials (wood, stone, brick, and metal) and in a variety of combinations (small, large, straight, curved, open, covered). It is a bravura performance of inventiveness and sensibility, to my knowledge unmatched in recent landscape design.

---

18.   Two personal favorites are located in a park in San Antonio, Texas, designed and hand-built by a Japanese immigrant, Kimi Eizo Jingu, in the 1920s and 30s, and a tree house and bridge concocted for the Château de Blois on the Loire in France in the late 19th century.

19.   Dumbarton Oaks was created for Mr. and Mrs. Robert Woods Bliss in Georgetown; Farrand worked there from 1922–1950. Her other great surviving garden is the Abby Aldrich Rockefeller Garden at Seal Harbor, Maine; her work at Yale and Princeton Universities has been altered and degraded, and nearly all of her other estates and gardens on the West Coast and Atlantic Seaboard have been destroyed.

Contemporary commercial Adirondack chairs, Wellfleet, Massachusetts.
Graphite pencil on a sheet of coated paper, 1994

LAURIE OLIN

on the Beach at Saddell · Kintyre, Argyll · 8 August 2001 · Balmy evening after a day of grey, wet drizzle

sparkling sea today with gentle waves — fishing boats floating on the silver horizon. Sun on Arran

Folding canvas sling chairs, Saddell Castle, Kintyre Peninsula, Argyll,
Scotland. SB 126, pen and ink, 2000

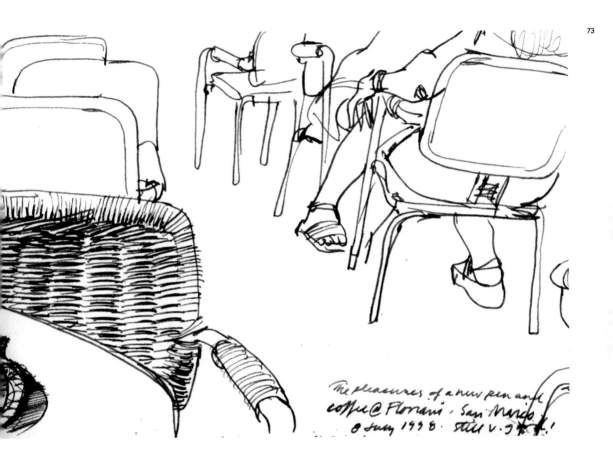

The pleasures of a new pen and coffee @ Floriani · San Marco · 8 July 1998 · still v. J.W.!

Traditional woven-wicker furniture has been translated here into simple industrial chairs of tubular metal and plastic at Caffè Florian in Piazza San Marco in Venice, Italy. SB 113, pen and ink, 1998

LAURIE OLIN

In general, however, in contrast to the inventiveness in furnishing 19th-century parks by the Olmsted firm, the 20th century witnessed an overall decrease in diversity of both material and style of park benches. For reasons of economy as well as aesthetics, a simpler design expression for landscape furnishings has prevailed in urban parks since the Great Depression; this was exemplified by the Robert Moses–era World's Fair benches in New York, which were made of standardized pre-cast concrete supports and pre-cut wooden slats.

In Philadelphia, as well as in London, Berlin, Rome, and cities around the globe, a standardized version of the English Mendip bench often became the default furnishing solution for parks and public gardens. As such they are often hardly noticed with their silver-gray, weathered tone, becoming truly part of the background, much like the ubiquitous squirrels of the same hue—something of a triumph of "ordinariness."

By the mid-twentieth century, a sequence of unexpected and unprecedented changes occurred that radically altered our experience of public places in almost opposing ways. The first had to do with the widespread dissolution of inherited wealth and property. World War I and the Great Depression had a devastating impact upon the upper classes in Europe, not only killing off a generation of heirs to ancient family estates but also wiping out the income of many families. World War II then brought with it more physical destruction—of cities, factories, and countryside alike. This meant that after the war, perhaps most notably in England, families could no longer afford their grand properties and were forced to throw their houses and parks open to the public for a fee in order to collect desperately needed revenue. A large number of famous English country estates, such as Montacute and Stourhead, became part of the National Trust; a great many others, while remaining private, became open to the public for visitation and recreation. (In one way this can be seen as a premonition of the alternative public/private alliances that would emerge to rescue parks and the public realm in many cities in America a few decades later.)

Strictly speaking, these parks are not public because there is a fee for entry; on the other hand, for the first time in recorded history, entry is possible. As a member of the National Trust, for example, a family has unlimited access to more than five hundred gardens, parks, and houses for less than ten pounds a month. Although galvanized primarily by financial necessity, this change has produced an enormous civic benefit. Some of the most beautiful gardens and parks anywhere in the world—Hidcote, Sissinghurst, and Stowe—originally designed exclusively for the private use of the aristocracy, are now open to the general public for their use and pleasure as part of their own patrimony.

During this same period, however, also driven by financial necessity in combination with postwar political shifts, many cities and towns were moving in a less positive direction. Because of the devastation from bombing throughout a great deal of Europe and an urge for modernization and slum clearance on the part of victorious and hubristic America, vast portions of urban areas on both continents were cleared, replanned, and rebuilt. The results, especially in the supposedly civic spaces—much of which had been heavily influenced by the abstract architectural ideology promulgated by the French architect Le Corbusier and others—were often brutal and empty. Gone were the facilities, materials, and furnishings that had made the urban spaces of the late 19th century so humane and socially vibrant. This "brave new world" was the one in which I found myself during my first years as a fledgling architect in America, and to which I soon turned my attention.

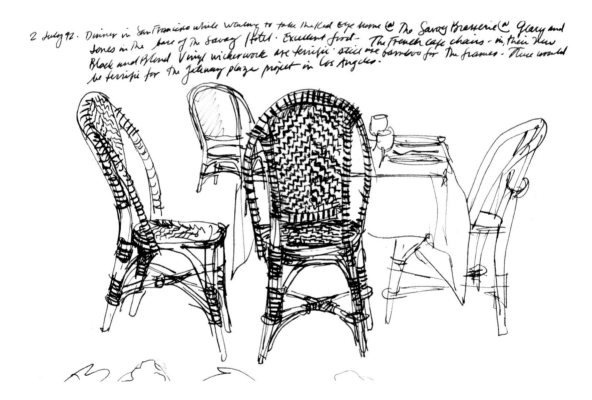

Contemporary French café chairs in San Francisco. Originally made of woven wicker and reeds, like a basket, today these are most commonly made of plastic, which not only makes them comfortable but allows them to sit outdoors through rainstorms without damage. SB 89, pen and ink, 1992

French Garden Luxembourg. Paris
30 May 1997

One of the problems of such spaces is
the incredible tangle of legs that one always
occurs most of these bases and backs.

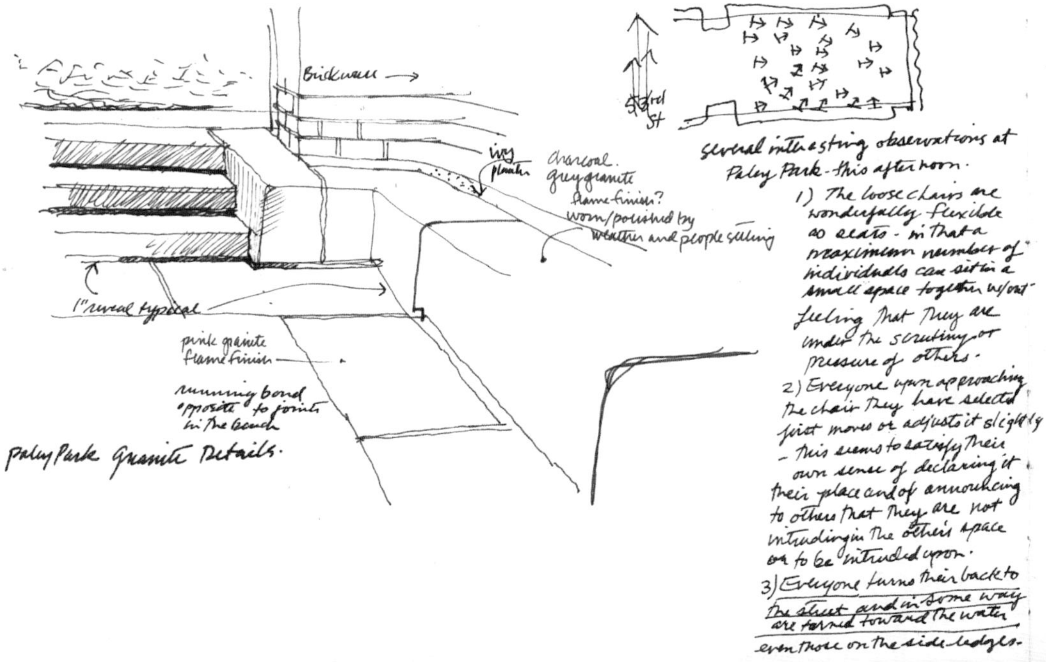
Brickwall
53rd St
ivy planter
charcoal grey granite flame finish? worn/polished by weather and people sitting
1" reveal typical
pink granite flame finish
running bond opposite to joints in the bench
Paley Park Granite Details.
several interesting observations at Paley Park - this afternoon.
1) The loose chairs are wonderfully flexible as seats - in that a maximum number of individuals can sit in a small space together w/out feeling that they are under the scrutiny or pressure of others.
2) Everyone upon approaching the chair they have selected first moves or adjusts it slightly - this seems to satisfy their own sense of declaring it their place and of announcing to others that they are not intruding in the other's space or to be intruded upon.
3) Everyone turns their back to the street and in some way are turned toward the water even those on the side ledges.

OPPOSITE PAGE Tables and chairs in the Luxembourg Garden, Paris: while the tables are a bit tinny, the traditional folding metal and wood chairs are heavier than most similar versions made and sold in the United States. Also, there is more of a pronounced curvature to the slats. SB 111, pen and ink, 1997

ABOVE Notes from a visit to Paley Park with a sketch plan indicating the distribution of seated people and their orientation toward the fountain and away from the street, along with a drawing of a planter wall that doubles as a bench. SB 47, pen an ink, 1982

Paley Park · New York · 15 Au

In midtown Manhattan's Paley Park, the light chairs designed by Harry Bertoia are complemented by the granite planter that forms a continuous seat. This arrangement—which recalls similar combinations of loose café furniture and wall banquettes in Viennese cafés—is one of the best examples of public seating design in recent times. SB 47, pen and ink, 1982

LAURIE OLIN

Discovering the Ordinary

For some time, even before my first trip to Europe, I had been noticing the powerful presence, use, and transformation of ordinary things and events in works of art of all sorts, whether in the radical painting of 19th-century France, modern American poetry, or Japanese and Chinese art and literature. The cold plums in the icebox evoked by William Carlos Williams, the imperfect and bent bowls used in the Japanese tea ceremony, and the haystacks in the frost depicted by Monet all resonated with this sensibility. Furthermore, this appreciation for dignified and elemental aspects of the mundane seemed almost an underlying starting point for the work of certain contemporary architects whom I admired, such as Frank Lloyd Wright and Alvar Aalto.

My first jobs at architecture firms underscored this interest in a different way. It was not uncommon at this time for the better architectural offices to design most of the hardware and key interior furnishings for their projects. While working as a young apprentice at Bassetti & Morse—a leading office in Seattle, Washington—one of my first tasks was to design and develop furniture for a library we were building at Central Washington State College—tables, chairs, card catalogues, and shelving. It was not only my introduction to millwork, joinery, veneers, and full-size detail studies, but also to the ergonometric and structural issues posed by the ordinary elements found in the interiors we were creating. Later, after graduating from architecture school, I worked with a team at another Seattle office that—inspired by the example of designers such as Mies, Breuer, Saarinen, and Aalto—produced designs for beds, desks, shelving, railings, light fixtures, and hardware for their new dormitories and science buildings at Western Washington State College. This training was invaluable. While most of these products were not particularly distinguished, I learned to work at several scales simultaneously while also considering the practical needs of the people who would be using the places we were designing.

My interest in such things was hardly happening in a vacuum. Throughout human history, there are moments when a number of people in different places and professions all become interested in the same thing at roughly the same time. The 1950s saw a remarkable example of this, when architects, artists, and sociologists on both sides of the Atlantic developed an interest in vernacular design and construction. While at architecture school, I had been impressed by Sibyl Moholy-Nagy's *Native Genius in Anonymous Architecture* (1957), which presented barns and humble farm buildings as springing from architecture's deepest logic and emotional sources. At the same time I discovered a number of articles published by Aldo van Eyck on the communities and structures of the Dogon in Mali. A few years later, while living in New York, I saw the exhibition *Architecture Without Architects* at the Museum of Modern Art. Organized by the architect and social historian Bernard Rudofsky, the exhibition presented a cornucopia of elegant structures from around the globe executed directly in natural materials by people in what were considered "third-world," poverty-stricken, or "primitive" conditions. Many were quite beautiful.

Intellectuals in other fields, I noticed, were also pursuing an interest in "ordinary" matters of life and society that had previously escaped critical examination and theory. While still a student in architecture, in addition to hanging out with painters and poets, I also had pals in the philosophy department who were excited by the recently published late writing of Ludwig Wittgenstein and his focus upon "ordinary" language and meaning. Years later, when I began teaching at Harvard, I learned that across the street in Emerson Hall, Stanley Cavell and Hilary Putnam were continuing to explore the significance and structures of everyday speech in what became referred to as "common language" philosophy.

Cavell would eventually write that an important aspect of his work at the time when I was a student and just after was "to understand the appeal of the ordinary in the philosophical practices of the later Wittgenstein and of J. L. Austin, hence of the tendency they counter in Western philosophy, since at least Plato's cave, of seeking systematically to transcend or impugn the ordinary in human existence." He went on to say, "I sometimes speak of the task as discovering the extraordinary in what we call ordinary and discovering the ordinary in what we call extraordinary; sometimes as detecting significance in the insignificant."[20]

Unlike many of his peers, Cavell was interested in the relationship between aesthetics and politics. He was also deeply interested in the relationships between individuals and the group—especially as they were negotiated through normative means and devices and as influenced by social constraints. Without writing directly about public squares and spaces, he speculated about the perceptions of reality on the part of individuals and their use of common everyday things to mediate their relationships.[21]

An interest in the quotidian on the part of architects and designers like these authors and myself was part of a broader interest in alternatives to the status quo and the structures and behavior of government, corporations, and institutions. In both Europe and America, disillusionment and a sense of malaise were increasingly leading to action and protest. An enormous quantity of the buildings and urban districts that had been built hurriedly after the war on both sides of the Atlantic became serious, even famous,

20.   Stanley Cavell, "Companionable Thinking," *Philosophy and Animal Life*, Columbia University Press, 2008, p. 96. Cavell also refers in this essay to an earlier work of his, "The Uncanniness of the Ordinary."

21.   See the discussion by Sandra Laugier, "Wittgenstein and Cavell: Anthropology, Skepticism, and Politics," pp. 20-25; and Espen Hammer, "Cavell and Political Romanticism," pp. 164-170, in Andrew Norris, Ed. *The Claim to Community: Essays on Stanley Cavell and Political Philosophy*, Stanford University Press, 2006.

William H. (Holly) Whyte, sociologist and author of *The Social Life of Small Urban Spaces*,
speaking at a conference on civic landscapes at the University of Virginia. The others are
Elizabeth Barlow Rogers, the founder of the Central Park Conservancy and August Heckscher,
former Commissioner of New York City Parks Department. SB 66, pen and ink, 1988

LAURIE OLIN

social failures. A willful arrogance and lack of education and experience, a reductive formalism, naïve utopian beliefs, and ideologically based economic policies all combined to produce disastrous housing, vapid and anti-human public spaces, and dangerous streets and highways.

In response to these failures, a generation of young social scientists—psychologists, anthropologists, ethnographers, sociologists, and geographers—began to focus upon what was happening in cities, producing a number of critiques directed toward architecture and urban design. Jane Jacobs's *Death and Life of Great American Cities* (1961) led the attack upon the rationalist and mechanistic planning and design of the previous decade, arguing that the desire for simplistic and diagrammatic solutions had missed the richness and layered achievement of decades of urban life and growth. Jacobs believed in the intimacy and messiness of small-scale commercial and residential development; this was how urban life remained humane and citizens could keep track of one another for their mutual benefit and safety. Her view of cities began at the brownstone stoop or neighborhood corner store and built out from there—a bottom-up perspective on architecture, design, and planning that defended and celebrated ordinary structures and their unspectacular but healthy communities.

Jacobs's attack upon the establishment and contemporary transportation and urban renewal projects inspired a new generation of scholars and designers to take up the challenge of looking at contemporary urban environments and design paradigms in a new way. One of the most brilliant and influential of these was the landscape architect Lawrence Halprin, who was deeply interested in public spaces and how people moved through and experienced them. In his publications regarding cities and design, he devoted considerable attention to the qualities that make such spaces desirable—the textures, the light, the sculptural forms that engage the eye and spirit.

In large part inspired by his wife, Anna, a prominent modern dancer and choreographer, Halprin was preoccupied with questions of process and circulation. Highly conscious of both the theatrical aspect of public space and the aspect of performance in our communal and interpersonal behavior, he created designs that deliberately evoked echoes of classical and indigenous sites—of monuments, amphitheaters, and stairs. With his associates, Halprin also sponsored and managed some of the first public design workshops, several of which played a role in the creation of important civic spaces (these are documented in his 1969 book, *The RSVP Cycles: Creative Processes in the Human Environment*). In part influenced by dance notation, Halprin attempted to document the ways in which people moved through such spaces and what their visual and physical experiences might be. Others in the field also became intrigued by the challenge of not only trying to understand how people negotiated urban space, but also mapping how they did so.

Continuous and integral perimeter-bench seating and fountain at
Bethesda Terrace by Olmsted and Vaux in Central Park, New York. SB
48, pen and ink, 1982

LAURIE OLIN

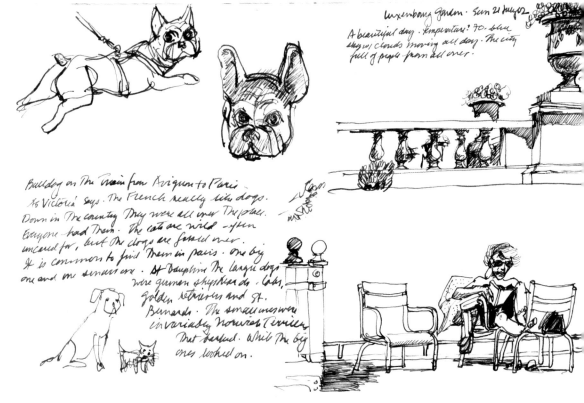

Luxembourg Garden · Sun 21 July 02
A beautiful day · Temperature: 70. blue
sky, clouds moving all day. The city
full of people from all over.

Bulldog on the train from Avignon to Paris.
As Victoria says. The French really like dogs.
Down in the country they were all over the place.
Everyone had them. The cats are wild — often
uncared for, but the dogs are fussed over.
It is common to find them in Paris. one big
one and one smaller one. At Dauphine the larger dogs
were German shepherds. Labs,
Golden retrievers and St.
Bernards. The small ones were
invariably Norwich Terriers
that barked. While the big
ones looked on.

An afternoon scene in the Luxembourg Garden showing how, when
it is not crowded, people gather up and move loose chairs to make
comfortable environments for themselves. SB 132, pen and ink, 2002

NEXT SPREAD Another contemporary variation on tradition—this
bent metal and wooden slat chair in the Tuileries combines several
precedents: that of Thonet's bentwood side chairs, the multiple wooden
slats of the Barcelona bench, and the comfort and light weight of
traditional Parisian metal and wood chairs. The square—not round—
tables offer an opportunity of being combined for larger groups. The
opposite page records a remarkable continuous stainless-steel, contour-
folded bench that forms both the coping for a fountain basin and
seating adjacent to the Pompidou Center. SB 111, pen and ink, 1997

LAURIE OLIN

Renovated café at The Tuileries · one of 4 now

nice metal and wooden chair. looks to be a stacking chair as well.

Eating light but area is easy here.

Breakfast. croque madame = welsh rarebit and a fried egg on top.

Lunch. Sandwich jambon with gruyère and butter on a superb fresh baguette.

evening. light repast @ Tingley + St. Phelle fountain place at Beaubourg consisting of

Tartare of smoked salmon, apples, celery and tomatoes, + pine nuts w/ toast points. or sliced lemon on the side w/ rusca dir

about have had good area on this trip in funny places street. in every case. full of ordinary French folk. reasonab

prices. modest, but very good food. They are amusing in groups. even fun.

Interesting
edging deta
beds @ The Tu
out curving
raised ab
adjacent
etc. w
lawn and flo

LAURIE OLIN

BE SEATED

Jardin Luxembourg · 21 July 2002 · Sunday·

People tend to pull loose chairs into a position where they can overlook
the action whether they subsequently do so or not, as is evident in this
sketch from the Luxembourg Garden on a sunny Sunday afternoon. SB
132, watercolor, 2002

LAURIE OLIN

One of my earliest sketches of public seating: an ordinary Monday
night at a trattoria in Orvieto, with the locals seated comfortably
together in view of the Duomo in inexpensive metal and plastic
chairs. The ubiquitous moveable furniture contributes significantly to
the relaxed and casual activity of the place, as it does throughout the
Mediterranean. SB 30, pen and ink, 1973

Kevin Lynch and Donald Appleyard at MIT—along with young faculty members at a number of design schools, such as Berkeley and Harvard—sought to re-engage cities on a phenomenological basis. Working from the perspective of the individual (which included personal experience, cognition, and visual, spatial, and temporal awareness), they encouraged a landscape-based framework for urban design and the creation of community. While Halprin was following his intuition and pioneering design workshops on the West Coast that placed emphasis upon one's own body—in part a cultural phenomenon of the 60s—Lynch offered a welcome corrective methodology to address recent dysfunctional and barren urban spaces such as the City Hall Plaza in Boston, publishing *Image of the City* and, later, *Site Planning*.[22]

Astute as these men were, however—and despite their great interest in streets, public space, way-finding, and the spatial structure and order of elements, buildings, and parks—they never got to the level of the physical design of the articles that people touch and sit upon. Like Halprin, Appleyard was beguiled by movement. Although he produced a fascinating work with Lynch, *View from the Road*[23] (which no one really knew what to do with), sitting still was the furthest thing from their minds. Car seats, yes. But parks and civic space, particularly seating and benches, were rarely part of their interest or perception at the time.

In 1968, an organization was formed to advance and disseminate such studies, the Environmental Design Research Association (EDRA), with the goal of creating and nourishing environments that would be responsive to the people who lived in them. (To this day, EDRA continues to advocate studies and research as well as to give annual awards to those who do exemplary work in this area.)

Following the upheaval of 1968 in France, Michel de Certeau began a series of articles that eventually culminated in *L'Invention du quotidian* in 1980 (translated as *The Practice of Everyday Life*), in which he explored how citizens resist the formal physical structures and direction of authority and corporations, instead adapting, co-opting, and rearranging aspects of the environment to suit their own purposes and convenience. His writing was particularly instrumental in shifting the focus of discussions regarding the environment from those who designed and produced it to those who used it and responded to it.[24]

As a creature of my time, when I entered the field of architecture, I too became interested in how people used things and how they behaved, and began to notice a number of aspects of the public realm that had been

---

22. Kevin Lynch, *Image of the City*, MIT Press, 1960; *Site Planning*, MIT Press, 1962.
23. Donald Appleyard, with Kevin Lynch and John R. Myer, *The View from the Road*, MIT PRESS, 1964.
24. *L'invention du Quotidien*. Vol. 1, Arts de Faire, *Union Générale d'Éditions* 10–18, 1980.

present for centuries but were largely unnoticed and unremarked upon, particularly curbs, pavements, drains, walkways, and seating. While I didn't have the vocabulary or theoretical apparatus to describe what I observed, I sensed that places to sit—particularly benches—were entwined with the spatial structure and social/psychological character and success of public spaces. And yet they performed their parts quietly, in several ways that were neither noticed nor understood.

Along with my colleagues in architecture and landscape architecture, I was reading a fair amount of popular and current scientific literature regarding animal and human behavior in relationship to the environment, such as Desmond Morris's *The Naked Ape*, Konrad Lorenz's *Studies in Animal and Human Behavior*, Paul Shepard's *The Subversive Science: Essays Toward an Ecology of Man,* and Rachel Carson's *Silent Spring*. It seemed fairly clear to me that one of the things that humans had in common with chimps and gorillas (not to mention lesser primates such as baboons and macaques) was that we were extremely gregarious and took enormous pleasure in one another's company. No matter who we were or where we lived—whether we were old men in cafés on Greek islands or a group of nannies with their charges in the parks of London, New York, or Beijing; whether we were teenagers at rural American soda fountains or Parisians debating in their sidewalk cafés—we invariably loved to eat and drink together while resting and watching others nearby. Men admired women on their lunch hour, society women studied each other's sartorial style in museum gardens, and teenagers, elders, and families on stoops surveyed the scene and the action, whether they were white or black, recent immigrants or descendants of the American Revolution.

While not quite knowing what to do with my interest in this scientific news, I happened to rent a studio in an old hotel on Skid Road in Seattle in the spring of 1969. I spent several months living there and hanging out on the streets, often sitting about in various situations with the homeless and winos, the down-and-out folks—it was an eye-opener. I soon learned how inhospitable most of the public realm was, regardless of one's economic situation. The well-to-do and middle class retreated to private spaces elsewhere, but the lower-middle class and the poor were bereft of any decent public space in which to come together. Despite this lack, they persisted in congregating where they could, sitting on curbs, steps, boxes, and the ground, creating a public community in spaces that were either ignored or unnoticed by the dominant society. I published my findings in a small pamphlet entitled *Breath on the Mirror* in the spring of 1972.

ABOVE A contrast in seated behavior at Sant'Eustachio, a highly regarded coffee bar in the center of Rome: on the left, two self-important businessmen (or politicians) engaged in negotiations; on the right, the languor and posture so characteristic of and perfected by Italian youth. SB 160, pen and ink, 2014

NEXT SPREAD Upper left: drawing of a wooden bench in Union Station, Denver, Colorado. Several aspects drew my attention: first, the end lamination of slabs of wood hung from frames that ended in tiny bun feet; next, the elegant and comfortable profile of their high backs; and, finally, that they enclosed steam radiators used to heat the waiting room as well as the benches. The other doodles are of Lawrence Halprin's Skyline Park in downtown Denver, which in his usual manner employed numerous ledges, steps, and walls for seating. The notes reflect suggestions for a possible attempt to save it prior to its subsequent senseless demolition, intended to drive homeless individuals from the area. SB 107, pen and ink, 1996

LAURIE OLIN

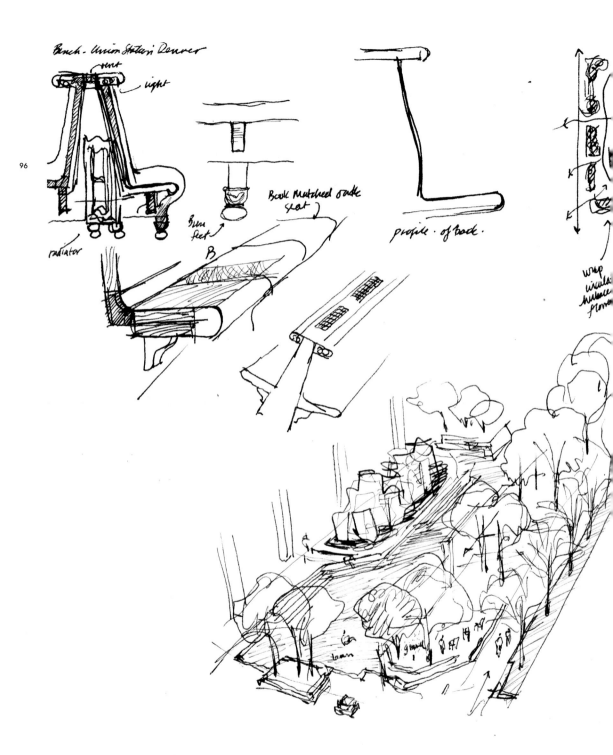

Bench - Union Station Denver

vent

light

96

radiator

Book Matched cradle seat

3mm feet

B

profile of back.

wrap circular buttress stones

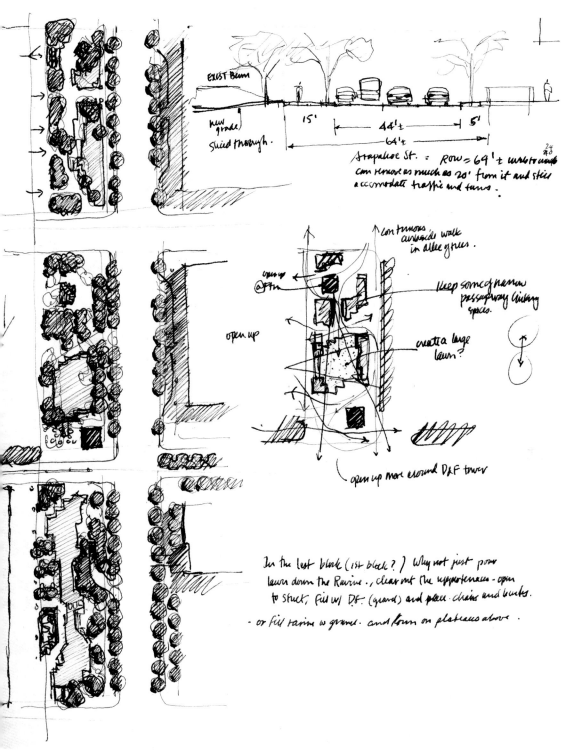

EXIST Berm

new grade
sliced through.

15' 44'± 5'

64'±

Arapahoe St. = ROW = 69'± curb to curb
can remove as much as 20' from it and still
accomodate traffic and turns.

continuous
curbside walk
in allee of trees.

open up
@ pm

open up

keep some of narrow
passageway linking
spaces.

create a large
lawn?

open up more around D&F tower

In the last block (1st block?) Why not just pour
lawn down the Ravine., clear out the appurtenances - open
to street, fill w/ D.F. (grand) and place chairs and benches.
- or fill ravine w/ gravel. and lawn on plateaus above.

A few months later, I set off for Europe with a dual mission. One was to study and write about my growing interest in the English landscape, which seemed to underlie so much of the pastoral tradition of American parks and gardens, in the hopes of coming to grips with its cultural and ecological history and future potential. The other was to examine the design and sociology of public space in Rome and other cities. A recent coast-to-coast trip through much of rural America and northern Mexico, combined with my growing interest in vernacular and indigenous design, had convinced me that much could be learned simply by looking closely at ordinary landscapes and spaces.

Frequently such places offered elegant yet straightforward formal resolutions to complex problems, and yet they were overlooked by the majority of the architects and planners I encountered in the offices and academic institutions of the time. My application to the American Academy in Rome posited that "the working mechanisms of a city are subtle and often unseen," and that the survival and success of Europe's great cities must be due to "intrinsic functional principles." It continued:

> My recent work has convinced me that emphasis upon the "Art History of Architecture" has often prevented us from seeing the more basic functional aspects of these artifacts.… I suspect that … people in a city that has survived as long as Rome live in a series of interlocking territories with all their physical and cultural requirements intact and that the aggregate of them has produced a vast multilayered organism very like a living forest. I would like to study the natural habitat of working- and middle-class Italians in Rome.

My time abroad allowed me to absorb an enormous amount of first-hand experience regarding Italian and other European civic spaces—not only their organization, design morphology, and activities, but also their physical fabric: the materials with which they were constructed and the details that made them emblematic or unique.

While I was living in Rome, the ubiquitous presence of people of different ages and incomes sitting about in cafés, piazzas, and *vicolos* interested me just as much as the behavior of people in Paris had. I came to realize that this was as much a function of the lack of sufficient interior spaces to support their needs as it was a positive choice. Many Romans couldn't or wouldn't invite others to their home or office to meet because these spaces were often too small, too shabby, or too crowded with others hanging about who would intrude or eavesdrop; or because they simply didn't wish to include others in their private spaces and allow them to scrutinize their possessions, in-laws, colleagues, or personal circumstances.

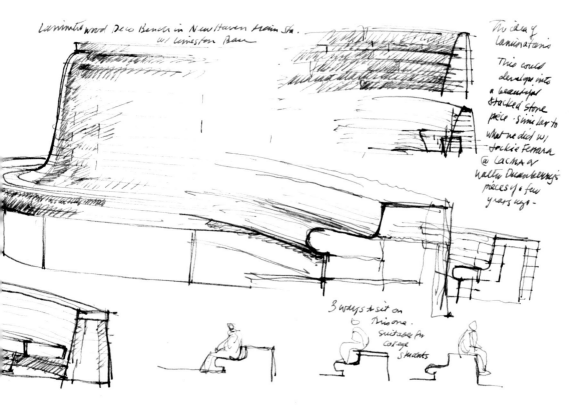

Laminated wood, Deco Bench in New Haven train Sta.
w/ limestone base

The idea of
lamination is
This could
develop into
a beautiful
stacked stone
piece - similar to
what we did w/
Jackie Ferrara
@ LACMA or
Walter Dusenberry's
pieces of a few
years ago.

3 ways to sit on
this one.
Suitable for
college
students

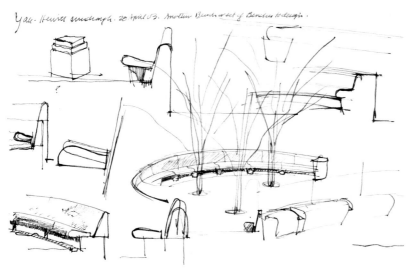

Yale. Hewitt Quadrangle. 20 April 03. Another Bench or set of Benches to design.

Study for a pair of wall-mounted benches at Hewitt Quadrangle, Yale University, reminiscent of apsidal benches in Hellenist antiquity, along with the above, a recording of the handsome and comfortable Deco-era benches in New Haven's train station. SB 133, pen and ink, 2003

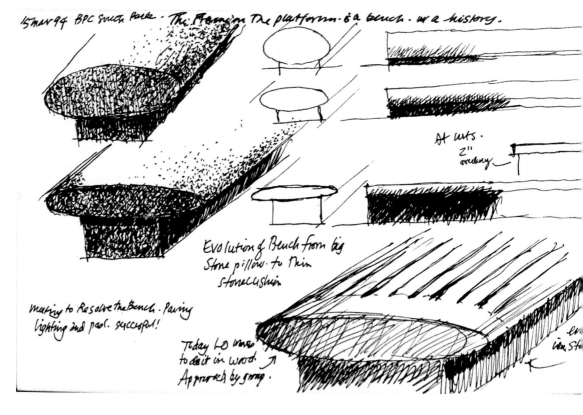

15 mar 94 BPC South Park. The Plantion The platform. & a bench. w a history.

At cuts.
2" overlay.

Evolution of Bench from big
Stone pillow. to thin
stone cushion.

meeting to Resolve the Bench. Paving
lighting and paol. successful!

Today LO wants
to do it in wood.
Approach by going.

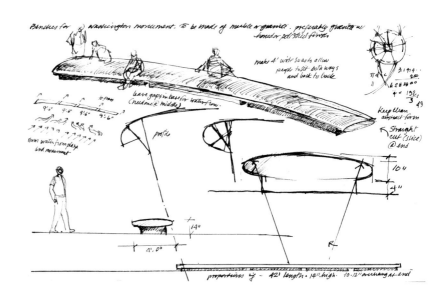

Benches for washington monument. to be made of marble or granite. preferably granite w
honed or pol. steel finish

make 4' wide so as to allow
people to sit both ways
and back to back

Keep clean
abstract form

Straight
cut (slice)
@ end

leave gaps in base for water flow
(needs in middle)

profile

form water from plaza
and monument

proportions if - 42' length. 14" high. 10·12" overhang at end

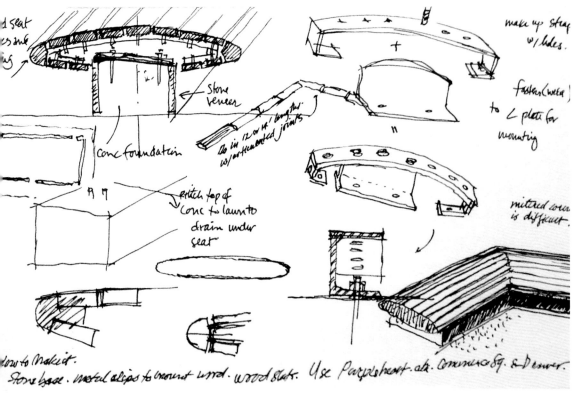

ABOVE Sketches recording the evolution of the benches around the lawn at Robert Wagner Jr. Park, Battery Park City, New York, depicting the shift in shape as it was transformed from the initial conception of them as stone "pillows" to ones made of wood. This choice of form and materials immediately led to considerations of fabrication and installation. SB 97, pen and ink, 1994

OPPOSITE LEFT Early study of curved marble benches at the Washington Monument in Washington, DC. This was a return to the stone "pillow" concept proposed for Wagner Park, and shows the first attempt to move surface water from the plaza through and beneath the benches and off onto the lawn of the hill. The later decision to set them upon a series of elliptical "feet" solved this problem elegantly. SB 132, pen and ink, 2002

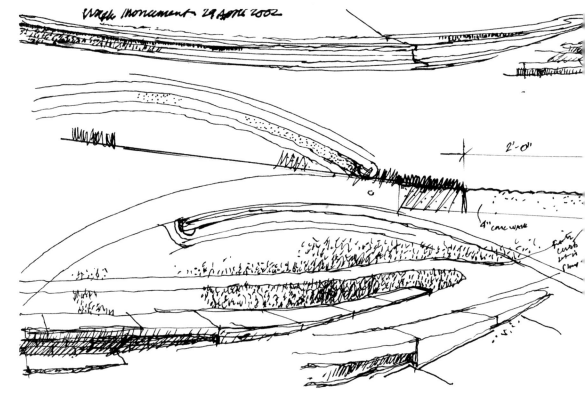

Virgil Monument 29 April 2002

2'-0"

4" conc walk

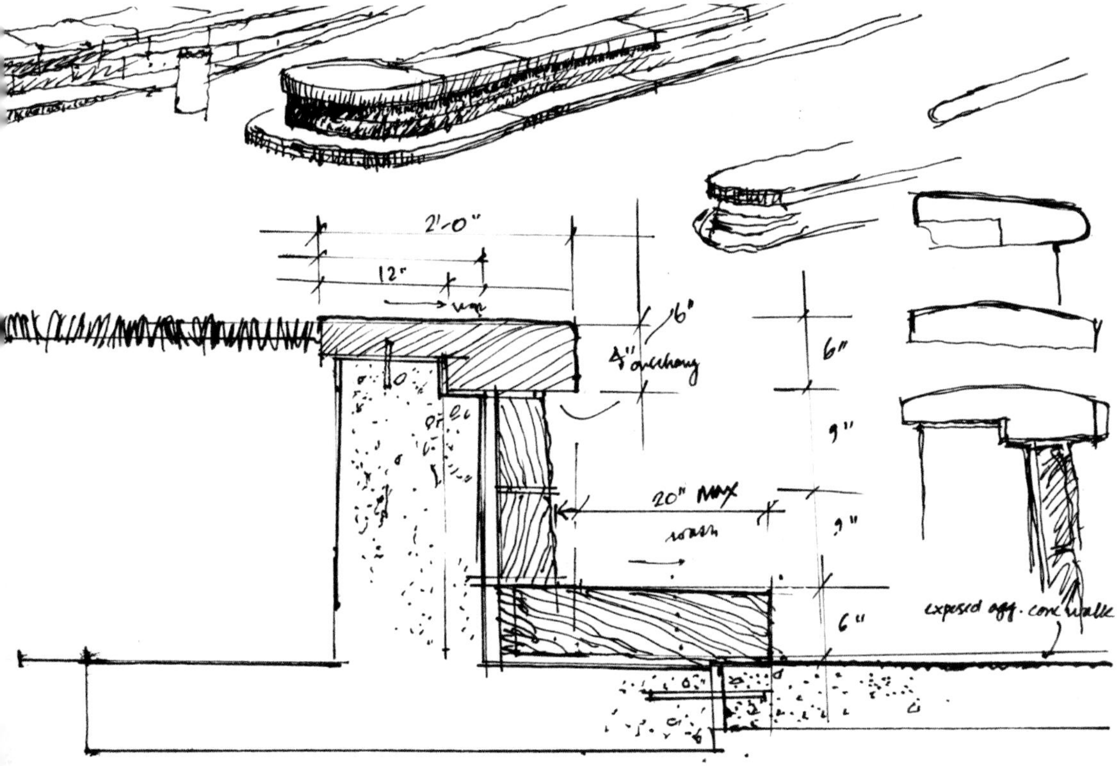
2'-0"
12"
6"
4" overhang
6"
9"
20" MAX
9"
6"
exposed agg. conc walk

Study for the anti-terrorist crash barrier at the Washington Monument in the nation's capital. A bumper/footrest has been added to allow the 30" wall to function as a seat, albeit a rather tall one. As usual, concerns regarding strategies for fabrication and construction can be seen as present from the beginning, along with other thoughts about form and composition and social use. SB 129, pen and ink, 2002

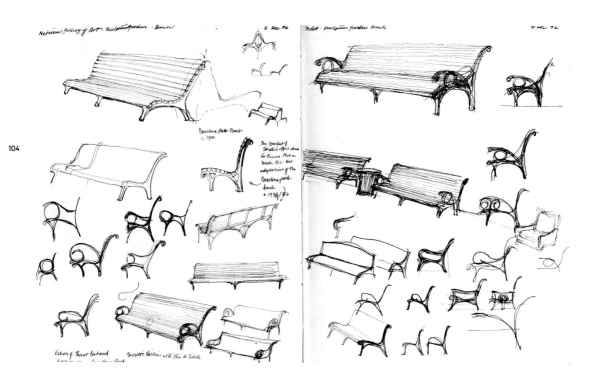

104

ABOVE Studies for traditional benches along paths in the National Gallery of Art Sculpture Garden, Washington, DC, that show concern for the context and earlier precedents while trying to relax the prototype somewhat. SB 109, pen and ink, 1997

NEXT SPREAD Studies of a custom bench for Hermann Park, Houston, Texas: various thoughts ranging from earlier prototypes, such as those of a favorite cane and bentwood café chair by Stendig, to traditional wooden English park benches and 19th-century iron and wood benches in Barcelona and southern France. SB 109, pen and ink, 1997

This meant that Romans carried out much of their private life, gossip, government dealings, love affairs, philosophical debates, commercial transactions, and familial counseling outdoors, in public—in and around the very café chairs, benches, ledges, stairways, and parapets that had caught my attention. By contrast, I realized, since the late-17th century, such activities in northern Europe—largely because of the climate throughout much of the year—had been accommodated within relatively public *indoor* spaces: teahouses, coffeehouses, cafés, taverns, bars, theaters, museums, and galleries.

Understandably, particular outdoor locations in Rome were populated by like-minded or socially connected groups: university students in one, senators in another, tourists here, neighborhood residents there. Given the vagaries of fashion and personality, the cafés and chairs in particular places such as those of the Via Veneto or Piazza del Popolo, once filled with cinema moguls and movie stars, were filled a few years later with American widows and business tourists on holiday, and more recently have been taken over by shoppers from the Persian Gulf and Asia.

The larger ecology—or sociology, as it might also be described—of the city and region that I'd thought I would write about faded as a manageable subject, but the life of these vibrant spaces and the forms and furnishings that supported it stayed with me. How people sat around and why in particular ways became an ongoing source of interest.

In 1974, the year I arrived at the University of Pennsylvania, Ian McHarg, the chairman of the department of landscape architecture, brought three anthropologists onto its faculty, in much the same manner that the department had enlisted natural scientists with foundation grants several years earlier: to give depth and a more informed and factual—even scientific—basis to planning and design. By 1975 a number of America's leading design programs (UC Berkeley, the University of Michigan, MIT, and Penn, among others) were exploring how research and the study of human physiology, psychology, and behavior affected their choices and the potential success of various design methods and solutions.

In addition to buildings, *public space*, especially parks and plazas, became a subject for social scientists. Numerous studies of varying quality and focus were generated. The cultural anthropologist Constance Perin, in her study *With Man in Mind,* made a case for methodically considering the urban environment at a series of scales: the room, the building, the block, neighborhood, district and city. Another well-known study was *Defensible Space* (1972), an examination of public housing and its ills by Oscar Newman. Not only architects and urban planners but also social scientists were studying American environments with the care and insight that anthropologists had previously devoted to remote indigenous societies—mapping, measuring, and studying the effects of design, both dysfunctional and otherwise—upon families and communities.

LAURIE OLIN

Hermann Park. Houston. Bench dilema. 8 April 97

106

← Better profile
Back too upright
Better angle →

Product of industry as is.
Landscape Forms. Such

Stiff and awkward looking

Side as is.

modification of as profile.
not right yet.

Also awkward, choppy. looking, stuck together look

the arm should somehow be integral to overall form and structure

Thonet Ch Stocky, no longer

could cross bench from it

in r. a b

English park Bench

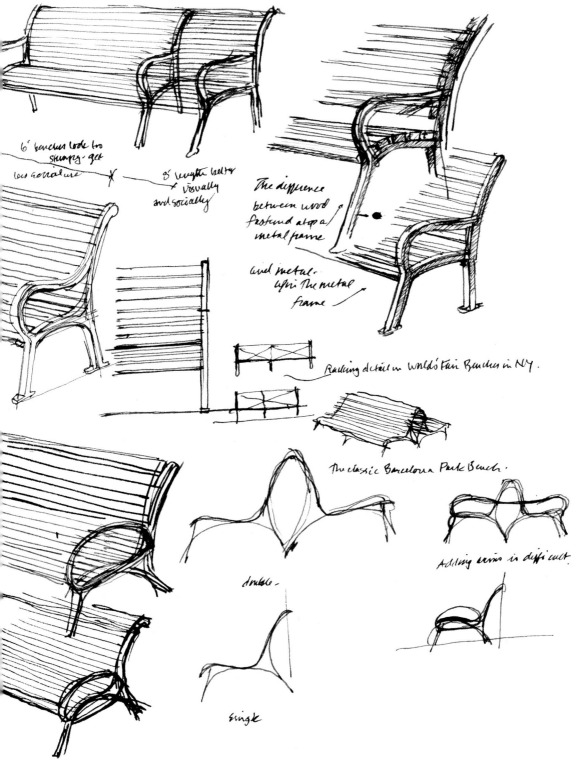

6' benches look too stumpy. get less variation ✗

9' length better + visually and socially

The difference between wood fastend atop a metal frame

and metal. upon the metal frame

Railing detail on World's Fair Benches in NY.

The classic Barcelona Park Bench.

Adding arms is difficult

double.

single

By this time, the observations of Jay Appleton in *The Landscape of Experience* (1975) outlining his now famous (if overworked) "prospect/refuge theory," combined with some of the behavioral study by Perin and Newman, had led me to conclude that *seating*—the design and arrangement of chairs, benches and ledges, steps and walls—was one of the keys to creating safe and effective public space. It was also clear that its setting or context (the floor, edges, and occasional canopies)—in short, the full expression that gives shape and character to outdoor space—was equally important to the success of public seating. While the field of landscape architecture includes so much more, regarding ecology, natural systems, and the planning and design of cities and regions, I became personally curious about the making of fine urban places for people.

And yet, despite an outpouring of writing and lecturing about urban design and fundamental principles on the part of architects in the 1970s, I couldn't fail to notice that the topic of seating was often overlooked—just as landscape architects like Kevin Lynch and Donald Appleyard had overlooked it in their admirable studies in the previous decade. One of the most extreme examples of this sort of omission can be found in the work of the architect and design theorist Christopher Alexander.

Following his inscrutable but dazzling *Notes on the Synthesis of Form*, in 1964, Alexander wrote a series of encyclopedic books on architecture and urban design that were at once poetic and highly descriptive – one might say tediously so.[25] Through several volumes he discussed patterns—what he describes as a "language" of design and construction—centered on centuries of human experience and accomplishment. He also provided numerous photographs depicting people lounging about on chairs, tables, benches, banquettes, and ledges, and even described the feelings derived from and the routine comfort of such encounters, and yet never in all of this writing did he actually mention or discuss the seats and furniture he chose to include. For all the pages of diagrams and photos, for all the rhetoric about community, civic space, comfort, health, and well-being that Alexander invokes, he never notices or comes to grips with the physical stuff we sit upon—not its position, its arrangement, its construction or its expression. As Ian McHarg once quipped, "Fish will be the last creatures to discover water." So too with most writers, scholars, and critics regarding the actual working parts of public space.

This curious blind spot was evident in practicing architects as well. Halprin, for example, although fascinated by kinetic movement in cities,

25.   Christopher Alexander, *The Oregon Experiment*, Oxford University Press, 1975; *A Pattern Language*, Oxford University Press, 1977; *The Timeless Way of Building*, Oxford University Press, 1979. This was true also of the earlier book he wrote with one of his professors from Harvard, Serge Chermayeff, *Community and Privacy: Toward a New Architecture of Humanism*, Doubleday & Company, 1963.

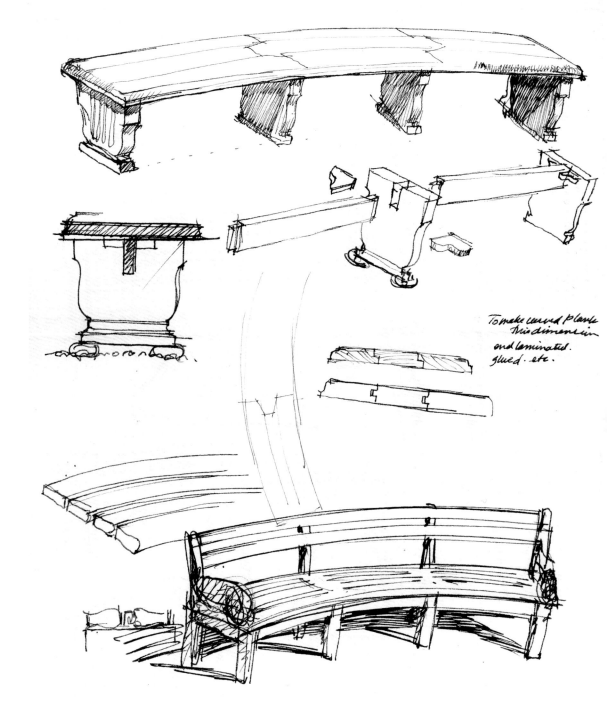

To make curved plank
this dimension in
and laminated.
glued. etc.

Studies for curved benches around a fountain in the Villa Aurelia gardens of the American Academy in Rome (unrealized). The gardens are in an Italian post-Renaissance revival style. The exploration in these studies involved the use of wood to produce low-key, relatively inexpensive, and easy-to-fabricate seating that would quietly fit into the garden. SB 107, pen and ink, 1996

LAURIE OLIN

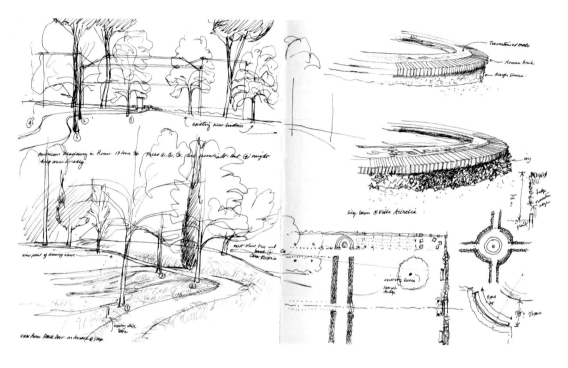

Study for the coping of a basin in the Villa Aurelia gardens, American Academy in Rome, intended for seating and an inscription. sb 107, pen and ink, 1996

barely addresses the question of where one might stop and rest in them. When conventional seating was included in his schemes, such as the benches at Nicollet Mall in Minneapolis and the Charlottesville Mall in Virginia, it tended to be rather simple-minded and crude. Larry didn't seem to focus on it.

In his greatest projects, however, such as the spectacular Auditorium Forecourt Fountain (now renamed the Ira Keller Fountain) in Portland, Oregon, or one of his last superb creations, the Stern Grove theater in San Francisco, there are plenty of places to sit, but they are all built in as ledges, skillfully worked into the fabric that shapes and defines them, whether of concrete or stone. There are no detached benches or chairs cluttering the space—nothing to move or break—just the space and its bones. One doesn't miss the normal furniture as the spaces are complete: people love them and sit about in them happily.

The two individuals who had the most to say about people and sitting in public spaces during this period were both sociologists: William H. (Holly) Whyte, in New York, and Clare Cooper Marcus at Berkeley. Whyte brought out a small book and film, *The Social Life of Small Urban Spaces,* in 1980.[26] Based upon several years of patient stop-motion film surveillance and mapping of public spaces in New York, Washington, DC, and other cities, Whyte made several original and insightful observations about social behavior. He pointed out how people walked, met, conversed, interacted, and relaxed in public, noting environmental factors that supported or hindered their actions.

Much of what he documented and pointed out was simply common sense, but some of it was surprising. His conclusions were clear, articulate, and delivered in witty and accessible language with incontrovertible visual proof. Central to his work was studying how and why people sat where they did. He produced measurements and statistics that eventually led to proposals to change the New York City zoning code to require a minimum quantity of seating in public spaces, most of it couched in terms of benches, ledges, steps, or (seat) walls.

Clare Marcus's work consisted of the methodical study of parks and community spaces in both residential and commercial urban areas. These studies—which Marcus undertook with the aid of a generation of her students at the Berkeley campus of the University of California—emphasize not the designers' intentions but instead the "post occupancy evaluation" (POE) of the designs based on her mapping of the activities of people who experienced them. Her useful conclusions have been summarized in the book she wrote with Carolyn Francis, *People Places: Design Guidelines for Urban Open Spaces* (1993).

26.   William H. Whyte, *The Social Life of Small Urban Spaces*, The Conservation Foundation, 1980. See also the PBS film of the same title, 1980.

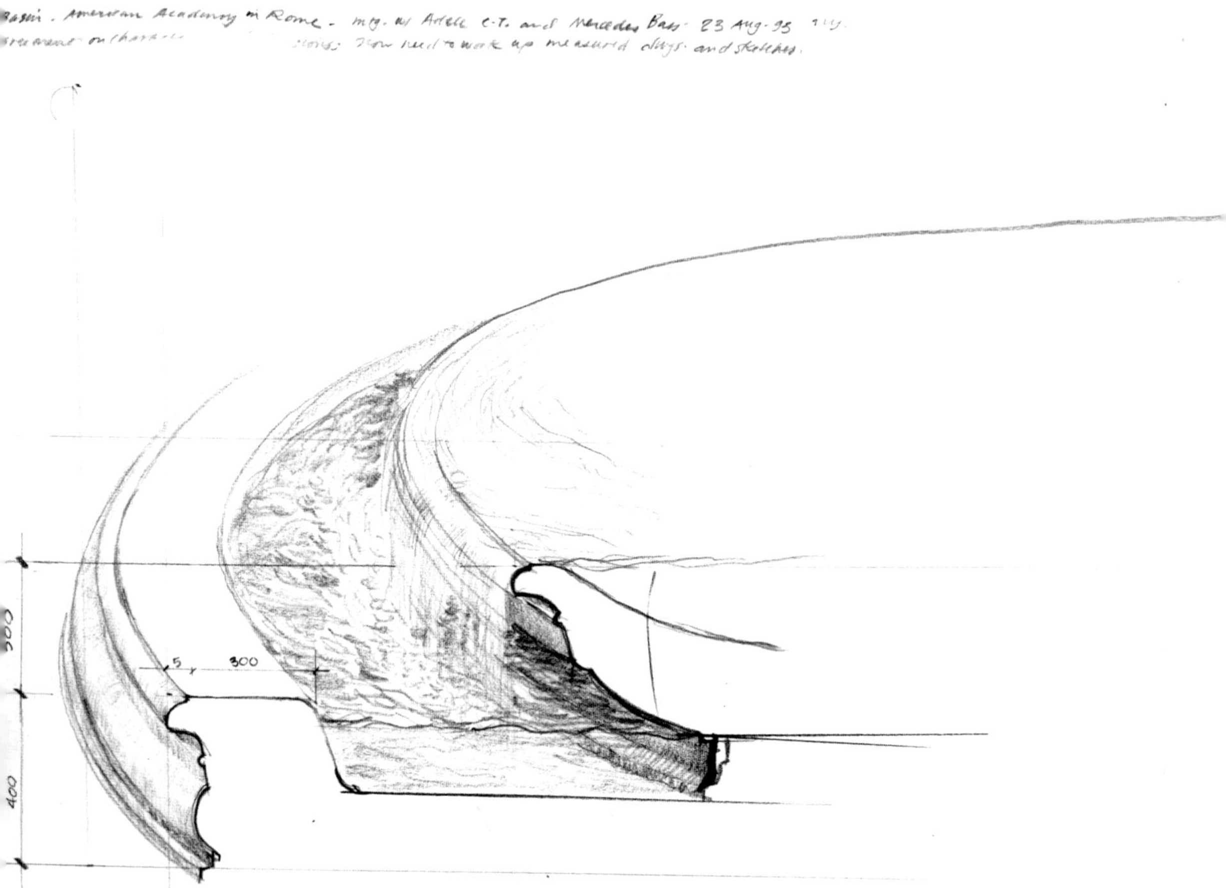
American Academy in Rome - mtg. w/ Adele C.T. and Mercedes Bass - 23 Aug - 95
need to work up measured dwgs. and sketches.
5
300
300
400

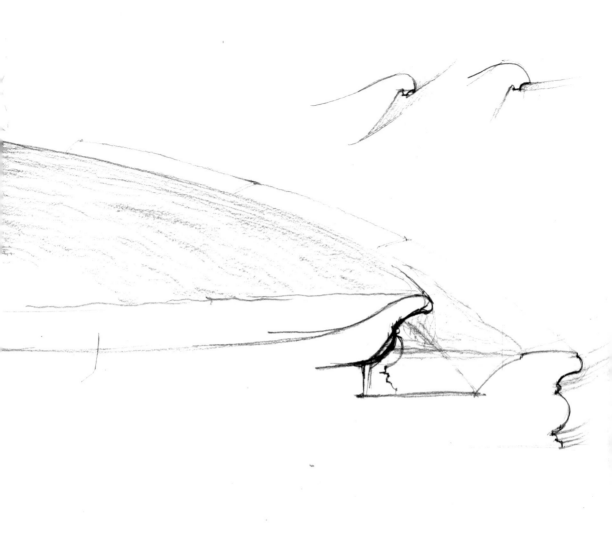

The basin rims of public fountains have often been conceived not only
to contain water but also to provide casual seating. This study led to the
Bass fountain in the entry court of the American Academy in Rome. SB
96, pencil, 1993

LAURIE OLIN

Knossos · Theater and Royal Way · 6 June 1980

The "Royal Road" at King Minos's palace at Knossos in Crete culminates
at an intimate rectangular amphitheater with a series of stone seats at
right angles to each other: a world made from stone and plants. SB 39,
watercolor, 1980

LAURIE OLIN

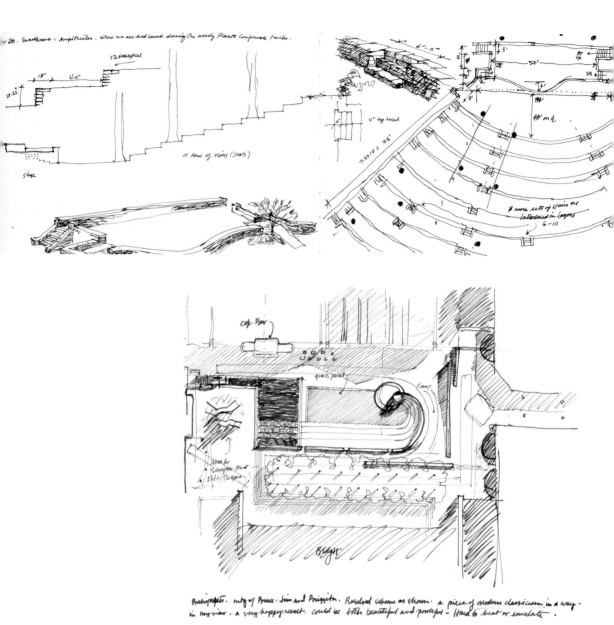

ABOVE, TOP A sketch plan and measured details of the amphitheater at Swarthmore College in Pennsylvania. The black dots indicate the location of tall tulip poplar and oak trees that the amphitheater was partly built around, as well as some that were added later. SB 150, pen and ink, 2009

ABOVE, BOTTOM Sketch plan of the rectangular amphitheater for Exchange Square in London, which summarized the key elements after a working meeting with the architects in Chicago. Broad seating trays face south across a small lawn into the open Victorian shed, where one can see the trains of Liverpool Street Station coming and going. SB 63, pen and ink, 1987

BE SEATED

Belatedly, Kevin Lynch took up more immediate sensory and social issues under the heading, "What For?" regarding the management of urban design by government in a later work. Using photographs of people sitting in Paul Revere Mall in Boston's North End and downtown Seattle he opined that "one could propose norms and standards for such things as … The availability to sit and lie down in public," following which he moves on to larger scale issues.[27]

Another profoundly astute observer of human behavior and activity in public spaces has been the Danish architect Jan Gehl. Unfortunately, although Gehl's wonderful book *Life Between Buildings* was written in 1971, it wasn't translated into English until 1987.[28] Like Whyte, Gehl devotes attention to the qualities of urban spaces and the properties that make them felicitous or not, whether for walking, socializing with others, or merely resting alone. He characterizes human activity in outdoor spaces as consisting of three activities: *necessary activities; optional activities; and social activities.* The first encompasses nearly all forms of movement. The latter often results as a function of the ability of people to pursue the second. Under the "optional" category he states succinctly: "These activities take place only when exterior conditions are favorable, when weather and place invite them. This relationship is particularly important in connection with physical planning because most of the recreational activities that are especially pleasant are found precisely in this category of activities."[29] When describing "social" activities, he notes that they "depend upon the others in public spaces," and matter-of-factly points out the obvious truth that "architects and planners can affect the possibilities for seeing, meeting, and hearing other people."[30]

27.   Kevin Lynch, *Managing the Sense of a Region*, MIT, 1976, pp. 17-20.
28.   Jan Gehl's *Life Between Buildings* was first published in Danish in 1971. The first English edition, published in 1987, was given to me by Catharine Ward Thompson the next year.
29.   Jan Gehl, *Life Between Buildings*, Island Press, 2011 (sixth English edition), p. 9.
30.   Ibid., pp. 12-13.

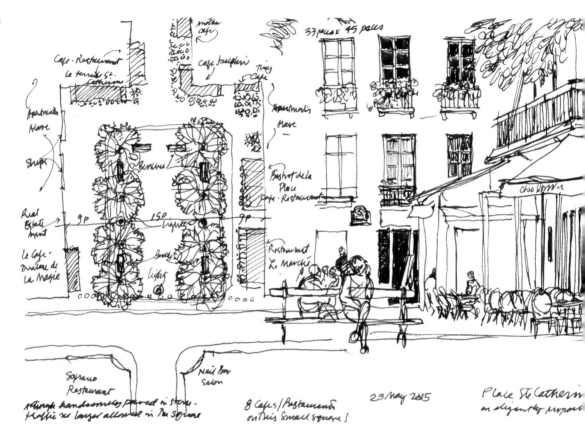

Café · Restaurant
Le Terrace St.
Catherine

another
café

Café Joseph

Tiny
Café

33 poules x 45 pales

Apartments
Above

Shops

Apartments
Above

Benvenu!

Bistrot de la
Place
Café · Restaurant

chez Joseph

Real
Estate
Agent

9 P

15 P.
Lights

9 P

Le Café ·
Théâtre de
La Magie

lovely
lights

Restaurant
Le Marché

Soprano
Restaurant

Nail Bar
Salon

Although handsomely paved in stone.
Traffic no longer allowed in the square

8 Cafés / Restaurants
on this small square!

23 May 2015

Place St. Catherine
an elegantly proposal

Chez Josephine

rais.
6+ story buildings. all around.

8 mulberry trees. 6 benches. 3 street lamps
and 8 (!) cafe/restaurants of varying sizes and ambition.

St. Catherine Place in the Marais, Paris, is a small urban square
remarkable for the quantity and quality of its urban life: there are eight
café/restaurants, eight mulberry trees, six benches, and three street
lamps. The buildings are uniformly six stories high, as is common
throughout the district. SB 162, pen and ink, 2015

LAURIE OLIN

Ramblas Catalunya. Lunch may 6. 1991. Barcelona.

BE SEATED

Streets traditionally were considered places for community encounters and social activities, not just for conveying hordes of vehicles as fast as possible. While the lower portions of the Rambla de Catalunya in Barcelona are largely devoted to shopping and strolling, the upper portions contain a number of cafés situated in the median, one of which is depicted here. SB 81, pen and ink, 1991

LAURIE OLIN

BE SEATED

Portland. Park Block 5. 19 Sep 06.

Among early concept sketches for Director Park in Portland, Oregon,
is one of a fountain basin and seat built on a slope, illustrating how the
fountain's water can be captured by a semicircular dam (or weir) that in
turn becomes a bench. SB 144, pen and ink, 2006

LAURIE OLIN

NOV 7, 06 Portland Park Block S.

ABOVE Moveable tables and chairs are shown in the space beneath a proposed high glass canopy on a terrace for Director Park in Portland. SB 144, pen and ink, 2006

OPPOSITE RIGHT Nighttime concept sketch of proposal for Director Park's sheltered terrace seating. SB 144, pen and ink, 2006

NEXT SPREAD A row of rockers for guests on the veranda of the Chalfonte Hotel in Cape May, New Jersey, the oldest hotel in the first seaside resort in the United States: Abraham Lincoln vacationed here during his presidency. Such porches were once ubiquitous across the country and allowed for social interaction in an unamplified era that moved slowly and more quietly. On this porch one hears the sound of the surf and gulls from the ocean two blocks away. SB 59, pen and ink, 1986

Porch of the Chalfonte Hotel.
Cape May, New Jersey.
The oldest hotel surviving in
Cape May (didn't burn down
w/ the rest of the town in 1860's)

In 1860s and 1870s, 3000 people
a day arrived by steamer at
Cape May Point, to stay for the
6 week season.

Built in 1876 this wooden
building is a remarkable
survivor of an earlier
era.

Noisy, creaky wood hallways
and stairs. Swinging louver doors
with no locks on the rooms.
No phones or television in any
of the rooms. Dim electric lights.
Straw mats on floors – it is as
close as one can come to another
era and a different, slower,
more personal way of life.
The sounds of voices and footsteps
of unamplified life are what one
hears. The sounds of the cooks
and staff in the dining room
rise to the open-screened doors and
windows of the rooms above.

Rows of rockers on the verandahs,
fresh paint on the deck and railings.
The sound of the sea two blocks
away, of gulls and the slap of a
screendoor and of voices. quietly
conversing, laughter.

This is justifiably the oldest
hotel at America's first
seaside resort.

126

LAURIE OLIN

As an architect, urban designer, and teacher, Gehl was interested in both quality and quantum, in several instances supplying dimensions and plans of highly successful social spaces in European cities. His considerations are those that seem obvious: sun and shade depending upon season; safety and avoidance of annoying or oppressive traffic; a good view to observe others whether they are walking past, engaged in activities, or seated nearby, etc. Gehl describes the situation and location of seating in a variety of spaces, but also uses observations and photos of people who are seated to explain numerous points about their social behavior without focusing upon their physical seats.

Another characteristic noted above and common to nearly all successful public seating—whether in spaces grand or humble, large or small, on pavement between structures or in the leafy domain of a park—he calls the *edge* phenomenon. Referring to the work of the Dutch sociologist Derk de Jonge, the English architect Christopher Alexander, and the American

sociologist Edward T. Hall, Gehl points out that it is within a liminal zone between two others that we commonly pause to evaluate situations; where we stand, linger, and sit around. Each of these earlier observers notes the commonality of the edge—whether it be of a forest or of a space adjacent to the wall of a building—as the model location for sitting, dwelling, and watching. Gehl offers many of the same examples, focusing upon the importance of position and arrangement, orientation and physical comfort.[31] Through lecturing, writing, and consulting, Gehl and his firm have had a positive influence on the design of public space and plazas in both Europe and America.

Porticos have been favored situations for observing life on streets and in squares for centuries. Native Americans from the Santo Domingo Pueblo and other communities sitting in the portico of the Palace of the Governors facing the central square of Santa Fe, New Mexico, where they sell their famous handmade silver and turquoise jewelry to tourists. SB 144, pen and ink, 2007

31.   Ibid. While examples and photographs of seating appear throughout the text, see particularly pp. 147-162.

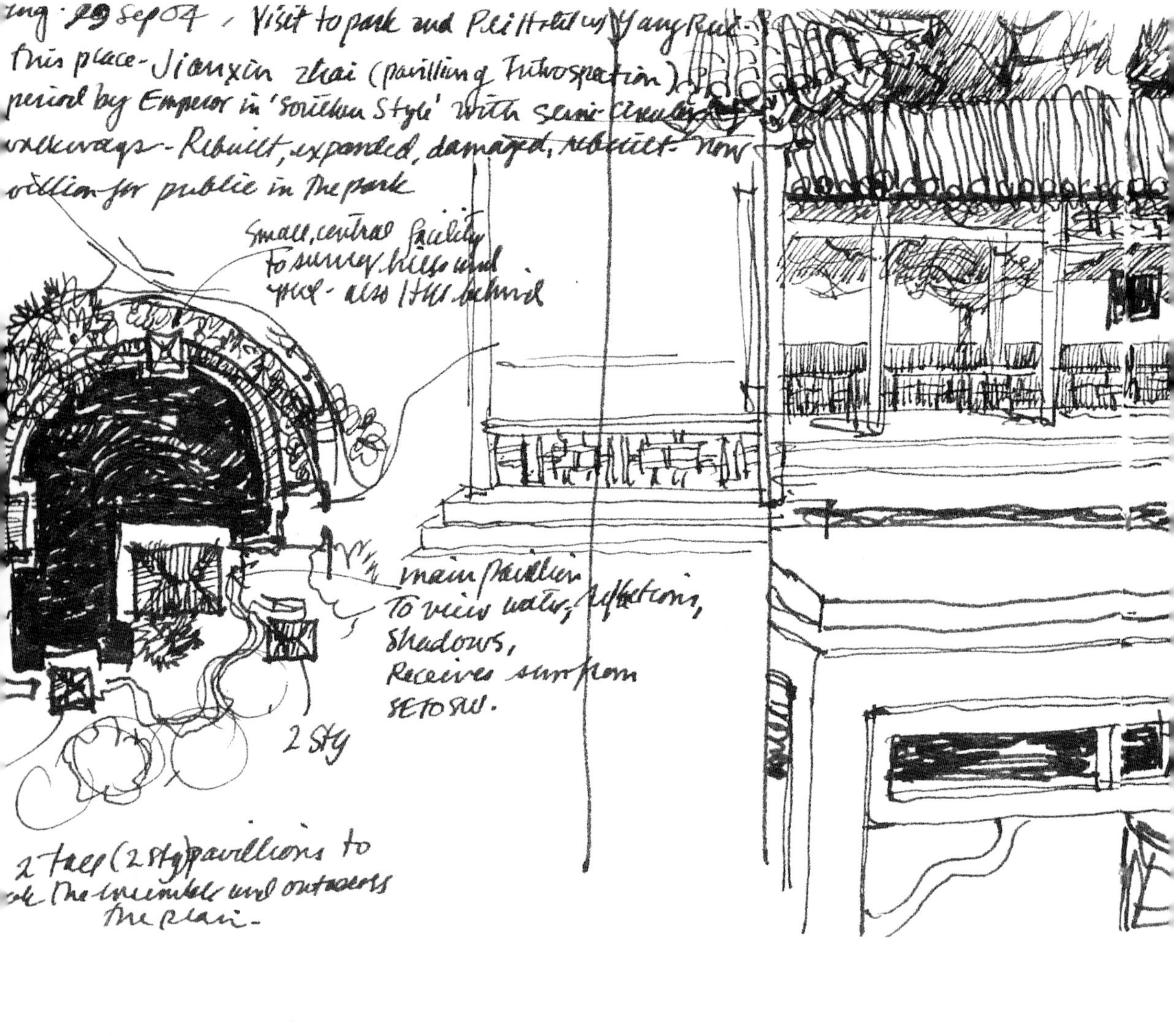

ing. 29 Sep 04 — Visit to park and Pei Hotel w/ Yang Rui.
This place — Jianxin zhai (pavilion of Introspection).
period by Emperor in 'Southern Style' with semi circular
walkways — Rebuilt, expanded, damaged, rebuilt. Now
pavilion for public in the park

Small, central facility
to survey hills and
pool — also Hill behind

main pavilion
to view water, reflections,
shadows,
Receives sun from
SE to SW.

2 Sty

2 ta[?] (2 Sty) pavilions to
see the ensemble and outdoors
the plan —

The combination of a continuous curved seating wall beneath a shade
structure, framing a fishpond and terrace furnished with handsome
wooden tables and chairs, makes for a superb café terrace at Fragrant
Hills near Beijing. sʙ 135, pen and ink, 2004

LAURIE OLIN

132

Yu Yuan. Built in reign of Emperor
Jiajing (1559) as a private garden of
Pan Yunduan a commissioner of Sichuan Province
2 hectares in extent. Extremely complex, rich, and
beautiful. At one point I was truly lost and
didn't know which way to turn to return
to any known area I'd been in or wanted
to go back to.

This year it's more advanced than last year
no plums were all in bloom plus the camelies.
The witch azel was finishing. There were bees out
and very busy in all the plum trees in both this
garden and in Ga Yi which we visited earlier
in the morning. 10. Mar. 05.

The willows were just breaking as well and gave
a delicate spray of color in both gardens.

This remarkable garden seat was created for Pan Yunduan, a commissioner of Sichuan province in the late 18th century, and sits in his extensive (two hectares) garden, Yuyuan, in Shanghai. It is a popular tourist attraction today. The seats in this pavilion are contrived to allow for friends and groups to sit together and converse, or for an individual to sit facing different directions, depending upon the season and time of day. When I visited, it was spring and the plum blossoms were just coming out—ample reason to pause and enjoy. SB 137, watercolor, 2005

LAURIE OLIN

I have often referred to the phenomenon that Gehl analyzes as the "inhabited edge." One of the best examples I know of is that of the populated liminal spaces of Bryant Park, discussed in more detail below. Other classic examples are those of the Campo in Siena, or Antoni Gaudí's remarkable curvilinear bench that encircles the elevated piazza of the Park Güell in Barcelona. Numerous successful esplanades around the world are favorable places to sit owing to their "edge" condition—literally where one has one's back to a building, street, or wall and faces toward an interesting or attractive open space, often a plaza, lake, or harbor. The stunning success of James Corner's Field Operations project on the High Line in New York City is in significant part due to the fact that the entire walkway with its seating is de facto an "edge" or liminal condition that can be inhabited, psychologically and physically.

Inexplicably, discussion or interest in finding out what people really do and need in public space is not often part of the curricula today in many leading design schools throughout the world, despite the large body of research and data on the topics that EDRA, its adherents, and others have generated. In addition to Gehl in Denmark and Clare Cooper Marcus on the West Coast, the landscape architect Catharine Ward Thompson in Edinburgh has continued to advocate original research and direct personal experience regarding behavior and public space. Thompson has conducted an ongoing urban spatial usage study with her students at Heriot-Watt University and organized conferences on the topic, publishing their proceedings as well as her own research, one example of which is *Open Space: People Space*.

So, too, a generation of scholars at the Bartlett School in London has participated in several decades of original research, concerning itself with both the physical and social structure of public space, especially pedestrian movement and wayfinding. Unfortunately, however, despite having influenced planning practices and regulations in Britain, most of this exemplary work thus far has had negligible effect upon the design of public seating in America.

RIGHT This small stool or hassock was in a hotel room in the former Casbah in Kairouan, Tunisia. Notice how the formal expression of this piece immediately tells you it is from a Muslim country or the Middle East. SB 147, pen and ink, 2008

Stool in the Hotel Room in the Casbah
at Kairouan - a fine Hassock.

LAURIE OLIN

Simple Truths in Plain Sight

Many of us who live in cities spend a lot of time walking about to accomplish daily routines; for a good part of the day, we are standing or moving. When people go into parks, squares, and plazas, however, whether big or small, they also like to pause and rest. This inevitably leads to a desire to sit, look about, watch the scene; to eat, read, or converse with others. This seems so obvious and natural that it isn't discussed or examined very much.

Most people don't spend a lot of time analyzing what it is in their life that works for them and what doesn't, even though they have strong unexamined reactions to the world around them that they act upon all the time. Designers, however, need to think about such things. Why do people sit where they do and not in other places? How do they sit when together or alone? Where would they choose to sit if they could? Some places seem comfortable and others are off-putting.

Despite differences in history and behavior around the globe, it is striking how fundamental and universal several of our preferences are. For centuries indigenous people everywhere have squatted ('hunkered') down, elbows on thighs parallel to the ground, or have sat, often cross-legged, directly on the ground, street, or floor on mats, carpets, or cushions: sometimes due to lack of available seating or simply from habit and choice. But Appleton was right. Regardless of manner, people *do* like to sit with their backs against something (a building, a wall, a mass of planting) and under shelter, if possible (a tree, a canopy, a portico, a doorway).

We also like to be somewhat elevated while sitting—a small amount above the adjacent space if possible. This is especially true if we are eating at a café. Most people don't like the food on their plates being examined by others walking by if they can help it. Partly for this reason many café owners in Europe (and recently in America) place an artificial hedge of plants between their outdoor dining areas and the sidewalk. Additionally, when seated in the shade, we like to look out into the sun and well-lit adjacent spaces to watch the movement and activities of those around us.

Appleton, Morris, and others have speculated upon our early origin in East Africa and how this sort of seating arrangement would well serve a creature interested in the presence and movement of herds or predators. The theory may be debatable but the practice is not: I have witnessed these behaviors all over the globe. Fraternity members on American college campuses, office workers in London and Philadelphia, and elderly grandparents in China all study the passing parade in comfort from just such vantage points.

That people in rural or wilderness areas perform rituals of community similar to urban residents shouldn't come as a surprise. Many Alaskans, whether ethnic natives or not, consider the natural landscape a publicly shared realm, as do indigenous people in many regions; thus the Yukon River is treated as a commons. Whether the Lenni-Lenape of the east or the Tewa of the southwest, American native people frequently had communal spaces in their settlements that engendered gathering and sitting. At the heart of Acoma Pueblo, for example, one finds conspicuous benches on the principal plaza of the town, which consists of a well-proportioned rectangular space between three rows of dwellings. Made of stone and mud plaster, these ample benches seat many elders on feast days, when the plaza is still used for ceremonies and dancing, but they are also perfect for sitting in the sun and having leisurely conversations.

By now many designers working in metropolitan spaces have absorbed the wisdom of William H. Whyte regarding the felicity of loose chairs: how one can move them into the sun or shade depending upon the season and mood; how they can be arranged by two or more people to support conversation or a group; how an individual can put two chairs together so that one provides a seat and the other a place for one's lunch or bag; and how an individual approaching a chair will often move it slightly, even if barely an inch or two, as an act of taking possession before sitting on it.

There are clear and straightforward phenomena regarding benches and ledges as well. For some reason benches in England and America for the past century have commonly been manufactured in two lengths: six feet and eight feet. From observation I can say with confidence that usually once one person sits on a six-foot bench it is deemed by others to be "full," and most people who don't know that person will look for another place to sit. Only when a park or plaza fills up and someone is already sitting on virtually every single bench will people begin taking less desirable seats on shorter occupied benches. Whereas if someone is already sitting at one end of an eight-foot bench, a total stranger will often feel comfortable enough to sit down at the other end.

This, of course, has to do with our sense of personal space—the bubble of immediate territory that we don't expect others to enter unless we are already on friendly or intimate terms with them. This distance varies from culture to culture, and also between individuals within the same culture. In Asia and parts of southern Europe, people are often more comfortable when close or even touching than are many in America or northern Europe. An exception to this is young people in a familiar group (a neighborhood gang, a clutch of students) who will jam together closely, almost atop one another, seemingly without encouragement and in good humor. Adults, however, whether on a bench or ledge, will tend to space themselves out—like seagulls on a roof—with a uniform gap of 2 to 3 feet minimum between them, even more if possible. Thus the longer a ledge or bench, the more seating it offers.

IMAGE ON P. 136 Our first experiment with moveable tables and
chairs on the 5th Ave Terrace of the New York Public Library, prior to
commencement of the Bryant Park redesign. Felice Frankel photo, OLIN

ABOVE A study of different uses and attitudes to the chairs in Bryant
Park: where and how they get moved about not only along the paths but
also on the lawn and upper terraces. Peter Mauss/Esto photo, OLIN

RIGHT Bryant Park in midsummer with the lawn temporarily roped off
for reseeding, rest, and recovery. Note backless benches inset into the
herbaceous borders. Laurie Olin photo, OLIN

TOP Olmsted-style park benches arrayed along the first phase of the esplanade at Battery Park City, New York, looking out to the Hudson River and the west. Peter Stegner photo, OLIN

BOTTOM Robert Moses-era benches, both with and without backs, under an allée of lindens on the first phase upper esplanade at Battery Park City, New York. Laurie Olin photo, OLIN

One also observes that, as at a lunch counter or a bar, two people can sit side by side and talk comfortably. Three people sitting side by side can still carry on a conversation if the middle person draws back a bit. Four or more in a line, however, immediately breaks down into sub-groups so that people can talk more easily. This is why continuous ledges and benches do not usually serve groups or families well, even though such linear arrangements can accommodate considerable numbers of sitters: people cannot see and face one another.

One must be careful not to become too dogmatic about rules, however. On hearing of my interest in how people sit in public spaces, an old high school friend instantly remarked, "My dearest memory of being seated is that of a big drift log on the banks of the Yukon where we all used to sit to watch the boats come in, or whatever. It was wonderfully companionable to be sitting in a line, though I can't think why." People's reasons for sitting where they do must also be taken into account. I'm sure that my friend's fondness for this particular memory had to do with the deep pleasure of sitting together with friends and watching the view. The satisfaction or comfort afforded by being part of a cohort has many dimensions, some of which have to do with seeing, and others with being seen. A line of construction workers on their lunch break, watching people pass by their work site, is one sort of line. But I also remember a solemn group of young black men I came upon sitting side by side on a stone retaining wall in Central Park the day after Martin Luther King was assassinated. They were not moving or speaking but instead bearing witness, by sitting in a line together in a very public place.

The possibilities expand when two linear seats form a right angle. L-, C-, or U-shaped configurations, as well as circular, elliptical, and square-shaped seating arrangements have been universally used to foster conviviality and community as well as for conferences and negotiations. Families and groups of friends gravitate to such configurations. As a corollary, one can observe people arranging loose chairs in such a manner to facilitate conversation and interaction. Likewise, dragging a couple of chairs up to a continuous ledge or bench can solve the problem posed by an inflexible straight line or configuration.

Curved seats, ledges, or benches offer another clear lesson. A perfectly comfortable ledge or bench that curves in a convex manner toward an adjacent space—i.e. one that bulges into it—is useful and acceptable to individuals, especially those who wish to be left to themselves for the time being, allowing a number to sit spaced out along it. Their solitary state is reinforced by the fact that, due to the curve, their backs and shoulders are turned away from any prospective neighbor—even if, depending upon the amount of the bench's curvature, ever so slightly. Conversely, benches or seating ledges that are concave toward adjacent circulation and open space are conducive to sociability because each person seated there is, to a greater or lesser degree, turned toward the others seated there. It may be very subtle, but it is operative. Families, friends, groups, even strangers are presented to each other in such situations in a manner that facilitates contact, friendliness, and communication.

The relationship between form and social behavior can be seen in other situations. Occasionally in parks or gardens one finds a bench encircling a tree. It signals "Come here, sit in the shade of this lovely tree." Doing so, of course, works well for a solitary soul, but the bench's small radius and pronounced curve render it hopeless for more than two persons to converse upon, even if they sit somewhat sideways. Such a form, however, is perfect for reading alone in a garden, or for 19th-century museums and bordellos, which favored multi-facing upholstered banquettes. The Renwick Gallery in Washington, DC, and the Kunsthistoriches Museum in Vienna still have good examples of such seating, the purpose of which was to allow sitters to focus their view upon particular paintings for a time, and then to shift to face different works. In brothels (for the innocent of today, such furniture can be seen in sketches and paintings by Toulouse-Lautrec and Degas), the goal was to allow male customers to view the prostitutes arrayed around the room without the embarrassment of having to stare at other customers simultaneously. Seating of this circumferential, outward-facing sort, like benches around tree trunks, allows one a measure of privacy and solitude while in the proximity of others.

For public seating then, it follows that the placement and arrangement of benches or terraces or kiosks or loose chairs can influence the way people feel and act in particular places. That said, people will often perch wherever they can if it suits their mood and need—on ledges, or steps, or bollards— and they will come to rest in remarkably variable positions. Many actually sit up straight with their legs in front of them, feet flat on the ground. Some sit on their legs, or leave one leg hanging toward the ground while bending the other in or stretching it out on a higher surface. Many people pull one or both feet back under themselves while sitting, even crossing their legs— especially if the seat is closer to the ground than the length of their lower legs. Many slouch and slide about in one direction or another. The clichéd cartoons of a teenager positioned upside down with legs dangling over the side or back of a chair are grounded in reality, at least in America.

Also, even when comfortably seated, most people unconsciously move and shift about every so often, readjusting their weight and contact so as to avoid becoming stiff or having one or more of their limbs go to sleep. While there have been studies largely driven by efforts to produce healthy chairs in which people can sit comfortably with adequate posture support for hours at a time for work—notable examples in recent times being those of two leading manufacturers, the Herman Miller Aeron chair and its principal competitors, Steelcase's Leap and Gesture models—to date such highly engineered, super-adjustable, expensive models have had almost no application in outdoor seating. The most common examples of adjustability in outdoor furniture have been deckchairs developed for ocean liners; poolside chaise longues; and the English canvas-and-wood park chair, with its sling seat.[32]

The issue of variability in the human physique has led to only a few rules of thumb regarding dimensions for seating, most notably that 18 inches is about right for the height of a seat for many people. After that, it truly varies. Experience shows that 14 inches will work too, and that people will hike themselves up onto a wall that is 2.5 feet high and let their legs dangle, but not often much higher. People will sit on stairs of all kinds, but the steeper they are the more comfortable, as long as the tread isn't too narrow for their behinds to gain purchase. On shallow stairs, people either have to stick their legs out parallel to the slope or have their knees hiked up almost to shoulder height. There are habits and principles for the design of seating but truly no rules, which accounts for why there has been so much experimentation and continual redesign of what seems a most ordinary problem.[33]

Another aspect of outdoor seating is the relationship between climate (mostly to do with temperature but also, to a degree, precipitation), materiality, and form. No one can debate that stone, metal, and wood conduct heat and cold differently. Most people have unwittingly sat upon a car seat that has been baking in the hot sun only to jump up or make a remark while adjusting to the shock of toasting one's behind. Likewise, metal, depending upon its thickness and color, can become too hot—or too cold, depending on conditions. Stone, too, can seem awfully cold and uncomfortable to sit on in freezing weather in winter. It is common knowledge that dark surfaces soak up heat and that lighter surfaces, being more reflective, retain less. In Arizona or New Mexico, therefore, one might not choose to use black stone, whereas I have done so for a seat and wall in New Haven, Connecticut, because a little warmth during the academic year there, especially in spring and fall, is very welcome.

This concern for comfort in all seasons, regardless of geographic location; lower costs; and the challenges of cutting, working, and shaping stone and metal have led to the nearly universal choice of wood as a

32.   This ubiquitous chair has produced a number of hilarious comic routines due to its somewhat tricky if supposedly simple adjustable positions: notable cinematic examples are those of Jacques Tati in *Mr. Hulot's Holiday* and Kenneth Branagh in *Much Ado About Nothing*.

33.   A recent landmark survey, the *Civilian American and European Surface Anthropometry Resource* project, measured the bodies of 4,439 people in North America, the Netherlands, and Italy, collecting a voluminous amount of data; in "Taking a Position on Plane Comfort," the *New York Times*, September 9, 2014, reported on the controversy regarding airplane seating and the difficulty of accommodating wide variations in human dimensions and preferences.

16th Street Mall in Denver, Colorado, after the restoration of moveable
chairs and the replacement and reorientation of benches to better
accommodate friends, strangers, individuals, and groups under the trees
along the central median. Laurie Olin photo, OLIN

desirable material for outdoor public seating. The popularity of metal for frames and structure derives simply from its strength in rather small dimensions and its malleability regarding the forms and shapes that industrial processes can produce.

In recent decades, various plastics have also entered the furniture world—in large part because of their light weight, strength, and formal possibilities. Most plastics, however, suffer damage from ultraviolet light and therefore age badly outside. They also scratch and can become shabby in ways that other materials don't. On the other hand, stone, wood, and even some metals weather from climate and touch and sunlight in ways that enhance their beauty.

As with everything else we make, there are fashions in the use and choice of materials. Sometimes this is the result of the discovery of a new material (one tropical wood replacing another, say) or a new industrial process (steaming and bending laminated wood) or a popular new design or personality (as exemplified by Edwin Lutyens's country house bench or Charles Eames' chairs).

Through the centuries, architects and landscape architects have favored stone for its durability and character, whenever they could use it for structure. Hence many walls and ledges, terraces and parapets, have been in stone while benches have commonly been made of wood. Since World War I concrete, due to its cheaper cost, has more and more frequently come to replace stone for public pavements, site walls, and steps. While often clumsily worked and commonly considered to be ugly, in the hands of good designers who pay careful attention to the sand and aggregate used, and to the formwork, surface texture, and finish, concrete can be truly handsome and elegant—even pleasant to the touch.

Just as walls, ledges, railings, and steps can combine to create successfully shaped and socially desirable places, they also allow people to gather and hang about in ways that can annoy or offend property owners or the general public. In recent decades, this tension has elicited remarkably negative responses on the part of city planners and designers, who sometimes now make these elements awkwardly high or uncomfortable to perch upon or even downright painful and dangerous, as in the case of adding spikes or broken glass. A war against the homeless and down-and-out members of our society waged by businesses, government, and a hostile or frightened middle and upper class has led to many negative actions toward public seating in American cities.

The most common antisocial tactic is to install an extra armrest in the middle of pre-existing benches that were designed and set out in a more generous era. The principal purpose of such armrests, of course, is to try to prevent people from lying down and sleeping. In addition to making the benches uglier, it renders them more difficult to use by everyone else for their intended purposes, diminishes the number that can comfortably sit on them, and sends a strong anti-social message. It also only works to a limited degree. I have seen numerous examples of people sleeping—no matter how uncomfortably or awkwardly—on benches with these extra "central" armrests.

This negative managerial attitude has also engendered another bad trend in public seating, which is to install tables and chairs that are fixed in position. Usually of metal, they are invariably awkward to use and hateful. In a naïve attempt to create something that is universal enough to work for most healthy adults, the seats are inevitably positioned too far from the tables, and the inability to adjust one's chair in relationship to the table, the sun, or one's companions is maddening. Ultimately, people don't like such arrangements and avoid using them if possible: the opposite of the supposed intent.

What many such failures in public seating point to is an absence of adequate (or any) management of the spaces. The foolish search for environments that are inexpensive, indestructible, and maintenance-free, unusable by the homeless yet still somehow purporting to serve a public purpose, has produced some of the most hideous spaces of the last half-century. Just as there is no free lunch, there are no maintenance-free environments, and there are few if any well-loved and well-used spaces that don't offer a degree of choice, physical freedom, and social comfort to their users.

Spaces not suited to attract and retain the middle class due to their poor design, lack of amenities (such as food, beverages, and entertaining events), marginal or inappropriate location, or poor maintenance and neglect are often overtaken by homeless and vagrant individuals, further insuring their avoidance and abandonment by society. Conversely, there are numerous examples of spaces that accommodate such people in distress but are also predominantly used by or filled with ordinary middle-class citizens—workers, shoppers, residents, neighbors, visitors—of diverse backgrounds and age. Bryant Park in New York, Rittenhouse Square in Philadelphia, and Director Park in Portland are all good examples of this, where homeless individuals are commonly present, but diluted in number and constrained in behavior by the self-monitoring decorum and civic influence of the larger crowd.

ABOVE High-backed, precast concrete benches and walls that also
provide parapets and screening for vehicular ramps to a garage below;
an ill-fated experiment at Pershing Square, Los Angeles. Laurie Olin
photo, OLIN

FOLLOWING SPREAD Refreshment kiosk with tables and chairs under
the London plane trees on a terrace in Bryant Park. Peter Mauss/Esto
photo, OLIN

LAURIE OLIN

From Appreciation to Action

I had returned to America to take a position in the Department of Landscape Architecture at Penn at the solicitation of Robert Hanna, a friend I'd made at architecture school in Seattle. Two years later, Bob and I had the good fortune to open a landscape architecture office together in Philadelphia. Along with my colleagues at the university, I was trying to digest various insights from the previous decade's ferment of research and theory regarding human behavior, comfort, and ecology while also pursuing my own interests in urban design and the history of civic space.

As our office began work on a number of ambitious urban and suburban projects, I consciously looked to the 19th-century work of Olmsted and Vaux in New York and to Alphand in Paris for precedent, believing that their example and inspiration would be of use. My interest was as political as it was aesthetic. Their designs, once deemed old-fashioned, now seemed less outdated than many of the failed urban renewal projects created only twenty years earlier, and their creations, when maintained, had proven to be both useful and sustainable for more than a century.

Their genius was in part conceptual: both Alphand and Olmsted could identify urban problems on a grand scale and imagine solutions that were commensurate in size. It was also administrative and logistical; they were able to establish offices and systems designed not only to execute their projects but also to devise ways that they could be maintained over time. And finally, their genius was in the details: these spaces were composed of and furnished with elements that facilitated social interaction, community, and value, both human and economic.

Two projects of our firm that were particularly informed by these influences were Bryant Park and Battery Park City, both in Manhattan.

In 1980, we were engaged to reclaim and "restore" the spirit and safety of the Fifth Avenue terrace of the New York Public Library.[34] A long, narrow rectangle above the street but below the building's actual entry, it had become a hangout for drug dealers and the indigent.

I was immediately struck by how French it all was, from the magnificent Carrère and Hastings Beaux Arts-style building to the entire vocabulary of the landscape setting. In fact, many of the site elements seemed to be direct quotes from the Jardin Luxembourg, a park I knew well and was particularly fond of. What seemed to be missing most was the quantity of seating to be found in the Tuileries and the Luxembourg; both the terrace in front of the library and the park behind it had only a few Moses-era benches to sit on.

My first thought was to experiment with this small urban place as a focused essay on civic space. Inspired by what I'd seen in France and Italy, I proposed to rip out the overgrown plantings next to the building, restore

OPPOSITE LEFT A version of the ubiquitous Mendip bench used in conjunction with the herbaceous planting in the side gardens of Robert Wagner Jr. Park at Battery Park City in Lower Manhattan, New York. Joel Katz photo, OLIN

---

34.   See J. William Thompson, *The Rebirth of Bryant Park*, Spacemaker Press, 1997.

One of the broad wooden benches in the shape of a pillow framing the lawn terrace at Robert Wagner Jr. Park that have proved popular for seating throughout the day and into the evening, Robert Wagner Jr. Park, Battery Park City, New York. Lucinda Sanders photo, OLIN

the pair of unobtrusive fountains flanking the entry, and create a simple but handsome stone-paved terrace with a tall canopy of trees. A pair of small kiosks with café tables and loose chairs would also be added, to serve light refreshments.

When I presented the design to the library, I expected some resistance to the notion of furnishings that weren't fixed in place. To head off such objections, I pointed out that there was at least one recent precedent for loose chairs in New York City. (Conservative clients commonly feel better if there is a precedent; heaven help the designer if something seems pioneering or untried.) I explained that such an arrangement had been successfully introduced uptown in front of the Metropolitan Museum of Art on Fifth Avenue when the sidewalks had been redesigned by Kevin Roche's office almost a decade before.[35]

To my surprise and relief Arthur Rosenblatt, the project manager for the library's restoration, spoke up in my defense, saying it was true that the chairs had worked out well. He had been the project manager for much of the reconstruction and expansion work undertaken by the Met before coming to the library. When others asked, "Weren't some of them stolen?" Arthur replied, "No, we do what they do in Paris. At the end of the day, we stack 'em up, throw a chain around 'em, and lock them up for the night." My proposal for loose chairs at the library went ahead.

When this small terrace on Fifth Avenue reopened, it immediately became a big hit. What had been a kind of no man's land hovering below the library and above the street was now a destination point: a new place to congregate in New York. The former drug dealers and panhandlers who'd dominated the neglected space before its transformation didn't return due to the steady stream of people coming and going and sitting about, eating, relaxing, schmoozing. The presence of the kiosk attendants and maintenance staff also guaranteed that the terrace was now both safer and better cared for than it had been before.

Meanwhile, the Bryant Park Restoration Corporation was trying to decide what to do with the much larger, equally significant, and far more troubled space behind the library. A once-loved spot in the heart of midtown Manhattan, it had more recently been nicknamed "Needle Park" and was plagued by drug dealing, occasional violence, sexual predators, and thousands of rats. Fortunately, just two years earlier, in 1980, William H. Whyte had brought out his small book and PBS film, *The Social Life of Small Urban Spaces*. It was Whyte and his research group, Project for Public Places,

35. Dennis McGlade of OLIN has redesigned the Fifth Avenue frontage of the museum, removing the Roche-Dinkeloo work. It was reopened to the public in September 2014, replete with fine pavement, allées of trees, fountains, steps, ledges, stone benches, and moveable chairs. Unfortunately, vending kiosks designed by the office of Rick Mather and OLIN were not implemented.

that subsequently carried out social use studies of Bryant Park on a grant from the Rockefeller Foundation and produced guidelines for its renovation.

Whyte recommended opening it up to the street while adding various amenities and uses such as food and beverage vending, ideas that were subsequently implemented experimentally by the Bryant Park Restoration Corporation. When these strategies yielded promising results, we were fortunate enough to be hired by BPRC to design the project. This led us to contemplate the theories and proposals of Whyte and others closely, learning by doing—which is, of course, the most effective way to absorb and understand many things.

Whyte's suggestions for amending New York City's zoning code were equally instructive for thinking about Bryant Park. A great proponent of moveable seating, he also cautioned that such chairs should be a complement to benches and ledges, not a replacement for them. As he specified for the code itself, "Moveable seating or chairs, excluding seating of open air cafés, may be credited as 30 inches of linear seating per chair. No more than 50 percent of the credited seating capacity may be in moveable seats, which may be stored between the hours of 7:00 PM and 7:00 AM. Steps, seats in outdoor amphitheaters, and seating in outdoor open air cafés do not count toward the seating requirements."[36]

Whyte wanted to insure that an adequate amount of seating would be truly public—that no one would be obliged to purchase refreshments to sit in a public space, or forced to sit upon the ground (steps, amphitheaters), especially in cold or wet weather. Among other recommendations, Whyte also discussed dimensions for the backs of benches and seats, but acknowledged that backless walls or benches, if wide enough so as to allow comfortable back-to-back seating, could be credited for double the linear quantum as required by code. He was also wise enough to know that what he was trying to do was establish *minimum* standards for ambience, and that places of genuine quality were often more generous, unique, and inventive, bending and shaping use and expectations. All these considerations would be critical to Bryant Park's success.

Looking back through my sketchbooks, I found notes from observations I made about Paley Park on 53rd Street that same year. This "pocket park" was one of the spaces analyzed in Whyte's work. Designed by landscape architect Robert Zion with the assistance of Preston Moore from I. M. Pei's office, it is an outdoor room the size of the town house that it replaced, with a handsome masonry floor and side walls covered in ivy. A grove of honey locusts pleasingly fills the space, and a waterfall covers the entire back wall in a frothy sheet. There are sitting walls on the sides, twin kiosks that form a

OPPOSITE RIGHT People relaxing and leaning about on the perimeter bench at the terrace lawn of Robert Wagner Jr. Park, Battery Park City, New York. Peter Mauss/Esto photo, OLIN

36.   Whyte, op. cit. p. 111.

Terraced trays of stone and turf forming amphitheater seating for the
view to the Statue of Liberty, Ellis Island, Hudson River boat traffic,
and the harbor at Robert Wagner Jr. Park, Battery Park City, New York.
Laurie Olin photo, OLIN

gateway from the street, and moveable tables and chairs designed by Harry Bertoia. It is probably the most imitated small urban space designed in the late 20th century. I took note of the seating arrangements:

1) The loose chairs are wonderfully flexible as seats in that a maximum number of individuals can sit in a small space together without feeling that they are under the scrutiny or pressure of others.

2) Everyone upon approaching the chair they have selected first moves or adjusts it slightly—this seems to satisfy their own sense of declaring it their place and of announcing to others that they are not intruding in the others' space or to be intruded upon.

3) Everyone turns their back to the street and in some way are [sic] turned toward the water even those on the side ledges.

Whyte got there first, and he got it right: today such observations are taken for granted by many landscape architects. But their significance is still not fully understood by city bureaucrats and the general public—as the bolted down seating in so many of our public spaces demonstrates.

When I considered the character of the historic underpinnings of Bryant Park, built by Gilmore Clarke in the 1930s, our Parisian influences seemed even more appropriate than they had to the terrace; both its organization and detailed elements were clearly modeled on aspects of the Jardin Luxembourg, and could be refined accordingly in the redesign. The park's orientation, however, had to be fundamentally altered. Whereas Clarke's aim—initiated in 1934, in the depths of the Depression—was to create an urban oasis, a retreat from the filth and chaos of the larger city, by 1982 the park had become overgrown, shabby, and turned in on itself: an isolated and dangerous place. What was needed was to open it back up and welcome the life of the city into it.

I decided to create more entrances to the park—two more on the north and south sides, respectively—and to rip out the hedges and recessed stairways to improve the sight lines from the street into the space, creating a far more permeable boundary and welcome feel. I also pulled out an enormous amount of shrubbery and ivy, which lightened the mood of the park's interior, and introduced gravel and loose chairs at both levels, as well as wide beds of flowers that could be seen from a great distance. The success of the Fifth Avenue terrace gave the BPRC board and staff, which were managing both, comfort that this was reasonable for the park as well, and we proceeded.

Before finishing, however, we needed to find another type of chair. Our original choice for the front terrace was marketed as the Rio chair. The

Stone ledges, steps, and a fountain merge into an amphitheater
providing ample seating for noonday crowds in Exchange Square on the
north of Liverpool Street rail station, London. Laurie Olin photo, OLIN

back and seat consisted of white plastic-coated square mesh supported on a thin tubular frame. They were contemporary looking, attractive, light, and airy. They felt modern, like the Bertoia chairs in the Museum of Modern Art Garden and Paley Park. Unfortunately, homeless people had quickly discovered that they could bend the back down into a horizontal position to align with the seat, and then, by putting two together, make a comfortable bed. Too many of the chairs were being destroyed. To remedy the problem, the Bryant Park Restoration Corporation next purchased a number of white plastic molded chairs. Although comfortable enough to sit in and easy to clean and stack, they looked and felt cheap and tacky. It was clear that they probably weren't going to hold up very long, either.

The chair that was found to replace them is now well known. Working on the problem, Rosenblatt located a supplier for a folding metal-frame chair with painted wooden slats for seat and back—similar to some of the Parisian park chairs that had been my inspiration. While not as delicate or up to date as the ill-fated Rio chairs, they were closer to the Gallic prototype. The color was also a consideration; we needed a great many chairs but didn't want them to register visually as clutter. Worried that the white we'd used on the Fifth Avenue chairs—or, indeed, any light shade—would be too obtrusive, I decided they should be painted the dark color we now refer to as Bryant Park Green.

BPRC started out with hundreds of chairs and they just weren't enough. It's a big park and New York is a big city. People often don't want to sit on the grass, and it would have been impossible to meet the demand for seating with traditional benches. Bryant Park, which once had no moveable chairs, now has thousands.[37]

In the last few decades, these light but sturdy moveable chairs have been introduced to other parks and public spaces all around New York as well. To differentiate the specific nature of these places, the chairs installed in them have been painted a variety of colors, from minty ice cream shades to more fluorescent hues. The vibrant red chairs in Times Square, for example, seem more in keeping with its dynamic jumble of traffic, crowds, and advertising, just as the deep green chairs seem apt in the park.

The rebirth of Bryant Park is widely known, and the importance of moveable chairs in the story has been repeatedly commented upon.[38] One measure of its success is the marked increase in the design and manufacture

---

37. There are now blogs and a number of internet entries regarding these and other related chairs and park activities.
38. William J. Thompson, *The Rebirth of New York City's Bryant Park*, Landmark Series, No. 4, Spacemaker Press, 2006; Cy Paumier, *Creating a Vibrant City Center: Urban Design and Regeneration Principles*, Urban Land Institute, Washington, DC, 2004; Alexander Garvin and Gayle Berens, *Urban Parks and Open Space*, Urban Land Institute and Trust for Public Lands, Washington, DC, 1998.

of park and café chairs that are competing in the ever-growing market for public seating. More recently the Bryant Park Corporation has even arranged to market a version of the "Bryant Park Chair," which can be ordered online, as a source of revenue for the park.

I've advocated the use of loose chairs on numerous occasions since Bryant Park, but only recently has this become an acceptable idea in other parts of America. Examples of our success elsewhere have been their use in an outdoor reading room for the Cleveland Public Library, on the plaza at Fountain Square in Cincinnati, and in Director Park in Portland, Oregon. This proliferation has in turn inspired emulation in the St. Martin's School precinct of the recent development at King's Cross and other recent parks in London, thereby taking a European tradition back across the Atlantic!

Another key to the success of Bryant Park, which should be common knowledge (but generally isn't), has been the remarkable management, maintenance, and programmatic activities of the BPRC, which continues to be responsible for its upkeep. Daniel Biederman, its original managing genius and continuing guiding spirit, would be the first to point out that this and other public/private projects that have succeeded since aren't simply the result of good physical design. Parks are imbedded within communities and must be managed like any other aspect of our world. Bryant Park is unique, but in addition to its strong physical design it offers management lessons that are invaluable.

One solution, like one size, doesn't fit all. There are times to experiment, and there are times to turn to proven methods. In 1979, for example, working with the architecture firm of Alexander Cooper, we began to plan and design the public spaces of Battery Park City in New York. When considering the first phase of the esplanade, I made a conscious decision to eschew invention regarding its furnishings, proposing instead to use items previously developed for the city's parks by the designers who worked under Frederick Law Olmsted and Robert Moses.

The reason for this was that there was a huge crisis of confidence in New York City in the late seventies. The city was teetering on the brink of bankruptcy, and much of its fiscal machinery had been taken over by New York State. The 90-acre landfill site had replaced a collection of decrepit docks and abandoned wharves in lower Manhattan adjacent to Wall Street, and yet the new schemes and plans to develop it kept collapsing in their turn.

One of the most serious questions facing us was how we were to produce a de novo portion of New York that could accommodate the contemporary attitudes and needs of its inhabitants directly adjacent to the oldest neighborhood in the city, whose strong and unique character had evolved over several centuries. Part of the answer inevitably involved the pattern and scale of the streets and blocks, and the massing and arrangement of the buildings and their uses. But part of it would depend upon its furnishings: the design, materials, textures, and elements of the pedestrian realm. When people stepped out of their buildings, where would they walk, and what would they see? What sort of surfaces would they touch and sit on? Finally, how much of this should feel old and familiar, and how much should be new and different?

As we began work with the architects on the master plan, Hanna and I examined the city's existing parks and waterfront esplanades. With the exception of Carl Schurz Park on the Upper East Side, which was built out on a deck over the FDR Drive, none of the waterfronts seemed particularly well designed, let alone inspiring. The terrace above the Brooklyn-Queens Expressway was superb in concept but almost too simple in execution. It was a nice place to walk, lean on the railing, and look at Manhattan, but it didn't have much seating at the time.

Battery Park City was a state redevelopment project, not the city's—in part as a response to the economic crisis. Even so, we conceived of the esplanade and public spaces that we were proposing as a de facto extension of the New York City Park system. As admirers of the work of Frederick Law Olmsted and the remarkable constellation of designers he had assembled in the 19th century, we studied the family of fixtures they had created. When combined with the furnishings developed under the parks administration of Robert Moses in the 1930s and 40s, they evoked "New York" and its public realm. I decided that we should adopt a mixed palette of these familiar elements, whether beloved or banal, to make clear that the buildings and public spaces of Battery Park City were meant to be an extension of the existing civic realm—not some urban Frankenstein, as the Pan Am and World Trade Center buildings had been viewed by many after they were built.

Along the water, where simple elegance seemed more important, we placed Central Park benches with their circular metal arms; on the upper walkway under the trees, we chose World's Fair benches of concrete and wood (with and without backs), both for their feel and to help keep construction costs down. Neither of these solutions looked particularly new or adventurous to anyone in the design community, but they worked: people came. The esplanade was almost instantly taken up as a legitimate, active, and attractive part of New York City—as if it had always been there.[39] Since then, benches have also been added to the Brooklyn Heights Promenade that echo the arrangement and style of those on the esplanade at Battery

---

39.   Peter Rowe, *Civic Realism*, MIT Press, 1997, pp. 192–195. Here and elsewhere, Rowe has written astutely about this project and strategy of ours and its relationship to the work of others, especially in Europe, in the creation of civic space—as well as the psychological/political and artistic issues involved.

A series of theater-scale ledges are gathered and pulled into the form of
an intimate amphitheater, Exchange Square, London. Laurie Olin, OLIN

Park City, further stitching these two places into the collective open space system and mental map of New Yorkers.

While Bryant Park and Battery Park City became highly successful public spaces, two others that I helped design in the same period had significant problems. These were the 16th Street Mall in Denver and Pershing Square in Los Angeles. One recovered; one has not, and may soon be demolished at the time of this writing.

In 1978, the year before the Battery Park City plan, we began work with I. M. Pei & Partners on an urban infrastructure project in Denver. Our client was a public/private consortium between a regional transportation agency and a local business organization attempting to revive the city's downtown. This thoroughfare for buses and pedestrians, which we conceived of as a Ramblas of sorts, turned out to be enormously successful in several important ways, yet for me it was a bit disheartening regarding public use and seating. The scheme consisted of only a few elements: a polychrome carpet runner of granite in a bold pattern (to differentiate pedestrian areas from two narrow bus lanes) and two rows of trees with unique and attractive lighting. This ensemble would extend for twelve blocks through the center of the city. Two fountains set flush in the pavement and enclosed by a circle of cube-shaped granite stools would frame the central symmetrical portion.

In addition to a pair of fixed benches in the median near the end of each block, I proposed that we provide loose seating in the form of several hundred chairs, as one finds in the upper portions of the original Ramblas in Barcelona. American planners—especially transportation planners— were absolutely uninterested in pedestrians in the 1970s, and the transit folks were very nervous about having a large contingent of pedestrians in the middle of a transit way, but the local development group, which was trying to revive the area for shops and restaurants, was game. We chose the same attractive Rio chair initially favored for the Fifth Avenue terrace of the New York Public Library. Here too, problems arose and the chairs gradually disappeared, leaving only the benches at the ends of the blocks. Unfortunately, the architects also persuaded our client to fix them in position diagonally opposite each other.

As it turned out, the transit/pedestrian-way worked handsomely. Large numbers of people came downtown to the mall. Business returned; commercial development flourished. Over time, however, groups of youths, along with a number of troubled, homeless, and drifting souls, also ended up on the mall. It was, after all, and properly so, a civic space, open 24 hours a day, and people of any sort were entitled to be there.

The right to peacefully gather and assemble in public is guaranteed in our Bill of Rights. Unfortunately, as mentioned above, in the latter part of the 20th century parks and open spaces in every great American city became the principal refuge for people who were homeless or otherwise in trouble, which in turn made these spaces contested zones. On the mall in Denver, the fixed layout of the benches exacerbated the problem. A small number of people could easily lay claim to a pair of benches (4 – 8 sitting, with others hanging about), often creating a noisy group that intimidated office workers, shoppers, and visitors walking by. This particular arrangement of benches and people also blocked easy passage along the central allée of trees.

To make matters worse, the granite cubes we'd placed at the fountains, rather than being seen as amusing and useful seating, turned out to be a hindrance to circulation and access into the central promenade space. This was when I learned that the precise dimension and placement of fixed things was just as important as what they were or how well they were made.

A number of years later, the local business community in Denver invited Project for Public Places, an organization founded by Holly Whyte, to make suggestions on how to improve the mall. Not surprisingly PPP suggested reintroducing colorful moveable chairs, installing art, and adding vendors, especially for food and beverage. Things improved upon doing this, but the problems created by the bench arrangement and fountain stools persisted.

Twenty-five years after the initial installation, the architecture and transportation planning firm ZGF from Portland, Oregon, and my firm (OLIN) were asked by Downtown Denver Partnership (DDP) to assist with the mall's restoration and refurbishment, and to recommend further improvements. Denver's preservation and architectural community, however, refused to allow us to alter the original paving, tree, and bus-way layout. The 16th Street Mall was theirs, and they considered it a "landmark." But they did agree to accept our recommendation to remove the fixed diagonal benches and awkward stone cubes and introduce more loose chairs, and to try omnidirectional platform seating that wouldn't create such blockages or encourage gang behavior. If one needed further affirmation that the arrangement of furnishings can affect social behavior, this 25-year-long experiment proved it.

Following the success of Bryant Park I was invited to join Ricardo Legorreta, the distinguished Mexican architect, to explore the possibility of redesigning Pershing Square in downtown Los Angeles. Essentially it was the roof of a multistory parking garage occupying a full city block in the heart of the business district. Once a luxuriant square, it had been ruined in the 1960s when a garage that was also conceived as a nuclear fallout shelter was built beneath it. Office space in downtown Los Angeles expanded exponentially in the 1960s, 70s, and 80s, largely filled with suburban Anglos who were moving into buildings further away from the square to the north and west, while Latinos and the businesses catering to them were moving in from the east and south. The Biltmore Hotel, once famous for hosting presidents, dignitaries, and movie stars, had turned its back on the square, closing its original grand entrance in preference for an auto drop-off a block away. Pershing Square had become a dividing line between the two dominant cultures in the city while accommodating a large population of derelicts and homeless—at that time, mostly aging men.

Working with a recently formed business community group, a powerful and enlightened real estate developer, and the Los Angeles Redevelopment Authority (RDA), Ricardo and I were full of optimism as we set out to design a place that would attract office workers, shoppers, families, and hotel guests from across the street. Imbued with hubris from the success of Bryant Park and Exchange Square in London, I proposed the incorporation of a café, kiosks for refreshments and vending, a lawn, a stage, a large active fountain in a paved piazza, shade trees, and plenty of seating—both fixed and moveable.

Thinking of both the climate and community, Ricardo suggested evoking aspects of parks and squares in Spain and Mexico. Chief among these were a series of colorful walls and long benches with high backs set under rows of shady camphor trees. These linear elements framed large open spaces with shallow changes in level and terraces of gravel or carefully colored concrete. We had fun working on the project; it seemed coherent, full of life and energy, a fresh place that could bring Angelinos together in the best sort of civic way.

The budget didn't allow stone, which would have been stunning, so we worked with several of the best concrete firms in America, and the project was handsomely built. We developed a series of precast concrete benches stretched into lengths that could accommodate many people. They were elegant in profile and beautiful in color and texture. Intended to accommodate leisure comfortably and to establish places from which to watch the activity of the square, they were one of its main features, positioned as a literal evocation of Appleton's prospect/refuge theory.

Thinking of examples in well-loved squares in Mexico, we exaggerated the height of the backs of these benches to reinforce a sense of security and containment, as well as to separate visitors from the traffic on surrounding streets and an unfortunate set of garage ramps we had been unable to eliminate. The resulting ensemble was visually attractive to us and seemed well received in the community at the time; a photo of the square was used on the cover of the *Architects' Guide to Los Angeles* soon after it was completed.

Unfortunately the public/private partnership intended to manage the square fell apart even while construction was underway. None of our ideas for playful corner kiosks at the entries were implemented. In the case of Bryant Park, a non-profit organization not only initiated, planned, funded, and built the park but has also programmed and maintained it ever since. At Pershing Square, however, the Los Angeles city municipal parks department—which hadn't participated in the square's inception, design,

People face in all directions on
the broad curving benches of ipe,
a tropical hardwood, Columbus
Circle, New York, City. Laurie
Olin photo, OLIN

or construction—suddenly inherited its ownership, management, and maintenance. None of the loose chairs we called for were furnished, other than a few in a badly managed and lonely café that failed.

With no food available, and no plentiful supply of moveable seating, it was difficult to build a new clientele for the space. Despite attempts to lure people in with noontime concerts and events, the Anglos didn't come down from their neighboring towers. Only a handful of Latinos came up from the vibrant shopping corridor of Main Street a few blocks away. The lack of people living rather than working downtown at the time also meant that there were fewer people looking for a park before or after the midday lunch hour.

Finally, our attempts to hide the sinister vehicle ramps on all four sides of the park with playful and colorful walls only compounded the problem, making the park less visible from the buildings, shops, and sidewalks across the street. In fact, this solution violated one of the fundamental principles of our own work at Bryant Park: namely, opening it up as much as possible. Intuitively I'd tried to do this by making overly broad entryways at all four corners of the park so that one could see in and enter easily, but it was still viewed as too closed and introverted.

Ironically, the design allowed the homeless and winos to feel safe and out of sight; they quickly returned to the square to discover the attractive and comfortable place we'd created, as if just for them. In an effort to discourage this population from sleeping and camping out, the city soon ruined the benches by adding an army of nasty metal armrests; this failed to stop the destitute from hanging out and sleeping uncomfortably there, but succeeded in making it aesthetically unpleasant for everyone else, as well. Public seating is always the first casualty in our society's war against the socially desperate.

Two blocks north of Pershing Square, adjacent to the city's main public library and in the midst of a group of office towers, Lawrence Halprin designed a small park, now referred to as the Maguire Gardens. Ironically, the property development firm Maguire Thomas that built it was also the patron for Pershing Square. It has several grassy berms, big trees, curving concrete paths, a number of active fountains, and a handful of heavy, six-foot-long commercial metal and wood benches. It also contains a major high-end café overlooking and occupying one complete side of the park with a busy walkway, fountains, and sculpture leading into the library. While it is never very crowded, this small park is well liked, and the homeless, who also attempt to occupy these benches, are generally discouraged from spending time there by both park employees and the LAPD. Occasional visitors to the library and office workers at noon in mild weather use the benches there as well.

In the past decade a significant number of people, especially young people, have moved into downtown LA. One result is that they are in need of services—schools, groceries, and places to take their children to play or to walk their dogs. The city now could use a good park there. At the time of writing, a non-profit public/private partnership of community, government, and business leaders called Pershing Square Renew has emerged and is working actively in an effort to rehabilitate the square through management and activities, enhanced maintenance, and restoration. PSR has sponsored an invited competition to completely redesign the square, a winner has been announced, fundraising is underway to blow up what one journalist referred to as the "widely loathed" park Ricardo and I designed and start over.[40]

The winning scheme designed by Henri Bava and his firm Agence Ter from Paris consists of a block-long pergola with cafés and seating, a large lawn, trees, and a generous fountain. The design is thoughtful, generous, and handsome in its elements, offering a simple repertoire of fundamental desirable elements and qualities—sunlight, shade, water, vegetation, amplitude, shelter, and openness. If, as seems likely, this new vision of Pershing Square is realized, the emerging community of families and workers living in downtown LA will flock to it.

The plans for Pershing Square suggest that both the city and the designers have learned from the mistakes of the past. A key feature of the new space is its elimination of nearly all the access ramps that have cut the square off from the adjacent streets and buildings for half a century. The toll exacted by the lack of management has also been recognized: certainly the aim is for it to be managed as carefully this time as Bryant Park has continued to be. Finally, there is still the question of seating. If people come and spend time there—whether it is to socialize with friends, watch some event, or have lunch or a drink—they will almost certainly do so sitting, individually or together. Exactly how this is to be accomplished is not yet determined, but in renderings from the designers one sees moveable tables and chairs of several kinds, plus long continuous benches facing out into the square. Ultimately, these unspectacular elements will be fundamental to the affordance and sociology of the square and its success.

Win a few. Lose a few. Civic design is always an experiment. But we should learn from our experience. While Pershing Square was a bitter disappointment, the rather heroic benches were still comfortable to sit on, despite being reflexively disfigured by bureaucrats. And their dimensions and proportions influenced subsequent bench design in our office, albeit in other materials, configurations, and situations.

---

40.   People other than the homeless have begun to return to the park, in large part because of a dramatic increase in residential development and conversions in the local area of downtown and a concerted effort by this new private group to sponsor events, art, and performances, along with making a number of temporary alterations to the park. How the city will deal with the conflict between this growing middle-class population and the homeless population still present will have as much to do with management as with any physical redesign and adjustments.

Peter Rowe has suggested that one of the tests for what he refers to as "civic realism" is the capability of our urban structures to reflect "many changeable aspects of society" and yet possess "a certain transcendental quality, by giving those in society a sense of something permanent in common." He suggests that there be enough of an architectural framework provided not only "to accommodate different functions, modes of behavior, and expressive proclivities" but also "to maintain a lasting and significant presence beyond those specific functions, modes, and proclivities." While Rowe was writing about architecture, civic space, and urban design at large, he has articulated useful measures for how we furnish our public parks and gardens as well. One of the most important tests of our urban spaces, he continued, "is an essential concern with everyday life and its depiction, and yet with a concomitant advancement in the art of a particular medium of expression." Finally, they must "provide for collective practices and rituals, while remaining congenial for individual habitation and experience."[41]

41.   Rowe, *Civic Realism*, p. 216.

Not-So-Simple Problems

Should benches for public seating have backs? This topic has provoked heated arguments between otherwise calm and thoughtful souls for decades. The commonly held view on the part of most designers and park administrators has been that benches in public spaces should have backs. Period. Certainly there is no question that a back on a chair or bench affords the most comfort for people who wish to sit and truly relax for more than a few moments.

In recent decades, backless benches have become unpopular for another reason. The rise of a large homeless population in America and their controversial presence in public parks and plazas have led to frequent endeavors on the part of authorities to prevent them from sleeping on the benches, walls, and ledges originally intended for seating. Backless benches so closely resemble cots or beds that public authorities and businesses frequently discourage their proliferation, whether they are appropriate or not.

Very often, a bench with a back is not only desirable but also essential. In the course of our practice, however, several projects have caused me to question their dominance, and to consider how best to produce generous seating in situations where backless benches seemed absolutely appropriate.

Despite having participated in what amounted to a movement to introduce moveable chairs into American urban parks, I have also devoted considerable energy to the design of fixed seating in the form of walls, ledges, stairs, and benches. I learned from studying Renaissance and Baroque spaces in Rome and elsewhere that fixed elements can be used to shape a space and give it particularity in a way that loose furnishings and off-the-shelf products cannot. Off-the-shelf seating may meet ordinances and encourage social use, but it rarely generates much order or form, and in many situations simply registers as too much clutter. A collection of manufactured benches, depending upon their design and arrangement, can seem stiff, militaristic, and antithetical to the sort of conviviality achieved by pulling several chairs together. Striving to find some sort of balance and to avoid doctrinaire solutions, I have often combined them, or occasionally explored custom-made alternatives.

My first such experiment occurred in the design of Robert F. Wagner Jr. Park, which effectively completed the Battery Park City esplanade and its sequence of parks. By 1992, we no longer needed to convince people that this site could be a legitimate addition to the public realm. What was required instead was a place that took advantage of its unique location at the southern tip of Manhattan. Seating and benches seemed the least of our issues as the design team grappled with matters of subsurface conditions; a program that included a café, public toilets, and maintenance facilities; and our client's conventional desire for trees, greensward, and colorful

OPPOSITE People seated in a number of ways upon the coping of the basin and the surrounding series of benches with their exuberant undulating backs, National Gallery of Art Sculpture Garden, Washington, DC. Laurie Olin photo, OLIN

planting: in effect, a public garden and park in what was, in some ways, an inhospitable location.

Seating, however, became a driving force behind the design as it became clear that the *raison d'être* of the entire ensemble was simply that the site was quite possibly the very best place in the entire city from which to view the Statue of Liberty, Ellis Island, and the harbor. Realizing that this small park was really a "room with a view," I shared a reproduction of one of Claude Lorrain's many paintings of a classical harbor at sunset with the client and team to discuss the situation. Here one would not only be looking at the sunset and the New Jersey shore but also, by implication, beyond it, to the West and the rest of America. The park needed to be a place to enjoy the immediate view and activity on the river and harbor but also one worthy of reverie and associative thought—and therefore a place where one would be encouraged to sit and linger.

The final design consisted of twin pavilions framing a view to Miss Liberty that also doubled as elevated overlooks; a terrace and broad steps descending toward the Hudson River; a lawn; and a pair of rich garden spaces set back from the harsh river environment. It called for seating at every turn, and, interestingly enough, each situation seemed to ask for a different solution.

Atop the pair of pavilions, visitors turn their backs on Wall Street and look out to the evocative panorama of the harbor. This elevated location demanded comfort as well as protection from a vertical drop to the entry plaza below. The architects, Machado and Silvetti, began with a traditional wood-slat bench on the roof of each pavilion. These they then modified, raising their backs up into what amounts to small walls to lean back on – strikingly reminiscent in form to the group of precast benches I'd earlier designed for Pershing Square, and for much the same reasons.

The side gardens below, while bursting with herbaceous material that one might find on an English country estate, are somewhat unconventional in their arrangement. Here we placed a number of familiar English-style teak garden benches—partly for their associative "country park" quality, and partly as a purposeful contrast to the modernity of their situation.

Closer to the river, we'd proposed a small stone terrace or piazza with giant stair treads leading down to the path and railing at the water. We envisioned tables, chairs, and umbrellas above and what amounted to theater seating, composed of broad stone ledges, below; here people could look out at the panorama of boats on the river, historic monuments, and the light of the ever-changing sky.

Originally the architects had suggested that I frame the upper terrace with stone benches, carved into a cross-sectional profile resembling that of a pillow or cushion. When we then decided to change this surface from pavement to lawn—partly for aesthetic and associative reasons, and partly as a cost saving—and to introduce grass on the broad trays below, I translated their idea for stone benches into ones made of tropical hardwood. We then framed the lawn with overly long wooden seats in a manner resembling the cushions of a billiard table, with gaps to allow easy access to the lawn. I made the seats three feet wide so that people could sit facing either way without interfering with one other. There were no backs to block the view of the water from the lawn or café off to the side, which we furnished with ordinary moveable chairs and tables with umbrellas.

People have draped themselves all over the expansive wooden benches, lawn, and grand steps ever since the park opened. The exaggerated wooden benches also act as railings to keep toddlers safely enclosed on the lawn, as parents and nannies face in to keep their eyes on them while socializing; others lie about and sunbathe, or sit facing out toward the harbor. In giving up one form of comfort, that of leaning back against support, we'd gained the enormous luxury of ample and comfortable space upon which to lie, sprawl, or sit about singly or in groups in near-infinite variations.

My next such experiment occurred nine years later. Following the terrorist attack of September 11, 2001, the National Park Service held an invited design competition for a solution to prevent vehicular assault on the Washington Monument that I managed to win. At almost exactly the same time, the Giuliani administration in New York decided to rebuild Columbus Circle to coincide with the anticipated completion of the Time Warner Center on the site of the former New York Coliseum at the intersection of Broadway, Fifty-ninth Street, and Eighth Avenue. As it turned out, both of these projects ended up with similar public seating solutions that have proved to be both aesthetically successful and extremely popular, contributing to their unique character and sense of place.

I decided that any scheme I developed to resolve the Washington Monument's security problem needed to enhance the monument's surroundings at the same time. Upset by the hideous emergency responses that had recently been thrown up on the sidewalks and streets of most American cities—especially around civic structures of importance and historic meaning in Washington, DC—I was determined to improve the public realm rather than wreck it. How might one take this sudden cascade of money intended for defensive measures and use it to leverage public amenity?

As part of our proposal I suggested cleaning up the site, relocating its surface parking, removing a nasty concrete addition to a historic structure nearby, adding and replacing missing trees, reshaping the hill, and repaving the area at the base of the monument. The Columbus monument in New York likewise needed a complete transformation.

The sites for the two monuments were, of course, radically different. One was atop a mound at the heart of the nation's capital; the other was in the middle of a five-way intersection, over the station for two subway lines, and next to several giant high-rise buildings and Central Park. Both projects, however, seemed to require public seating that followed the shape of the circular base of their respective obelisks. Furthermore, it was desirable for visitors in both places to be able to sit and look not only *inward and up* at the memorials but also *outward and away* from the vertical centerpiece toward the world beyond. The broad, backless bench with its somewhat elliptical cross-section that we'd settled on for Wagner Park seemed a good starting point for both—especially since for these two sites the benches would have to be curved fragments of a circle.

Early on I concluded that whatever seating we developed for the Washington Monument it must be of stone, probably granite or marble, in keeping with the surrounding Federal architecture, the setting of the Mall and Monument, and the new security walls and pavement we were designing. Additionally I knew that benches at both sites would need to accommodate the large numbers of visitors who arrived throughout the day and into the evening. In Washington, visitors have to wait their turn most weekends to ascend the monument. Many are weary from walking about the Mall, especially in the heat of summer, and need to rest. Seating was absolutely necessary.

This spot is also an excellent place to sit and take in the vistas and views to the Capitol, White House, Lincoln and Jefferson Memorials, and panoply of buildings of the Mall and Federal Triangle. The seating at one of the most symbolic places in America could not be domestic or rustic but would instead have to be in keeping with its inspiring vista and monumental marble obelisk. On the other hand, I was eager that it avoid the humbug and neoclassical bombast of the World War II Memorial and other recent postmodern architectural works in the capital.

I concluded that the monument's benches should be as minimal as possible. Recalling the elliptical cross-section and generous width of the wooden bench we'd introduced at Wagner Park, we built a full-size mock-up in the office and began investigating sources for marble. Along with my earlier decision that these curved benches would be backless to insure maximum vision in all directions while allowing people to stretch out and relax or sunbathe, I also concluded that there should be no vertical elements of any sort other than the monument itself and the ring of fifty poles with American flags (one for each state) that form a stylobate of sorts around it. We needed to avoid light poles, fences, or railings. It seemed that the seating should hug the ground, adjacent to the flags around the perimeter.

We settled upon a lovely, pale-gray marble from Tate, Georgia. The horizontal stone pillows that resulted—pure geometric forms vaguely reminiscent of classical moldings, cut as sections of arcs—were placed upon simple elliptically shaped supports that allow storm water washing down the monument and across the plaza simply to pass beneath the benches and run off into the grass of the mound. The warm reception to this scheme and the varied and constant use of the benches by visitors has been gratifying.

The monument plaza at the top of the mound wasn't the only place I thought we should offer a place to rest. The principal antiterrorist device employed at the monument—the *raison-d'être* for the project—is a set of low granite retaining walls that encircle the mound's base. Unfortunately, the height required for a crash barrier to stop a fast-moving vehicle intent upon damaging the monument turned out to be too high for people to comfortably perch upon. At the same time, Holly Whyte had conclusively demonstrated that low walls in the landscape make ideal people-watching seats. Given that softball games, events, and ceremonies take place nearly continuously on the lawns around the monument and that millions of people visit it each year, I was eager to find a way to modify these walls so that they could allow passersby to rest and survey the scene.

After considering several stratagems, I hit upon adding a hefty matching granite footrest along the base of the most opportune wall that faces the White House and Federal Triangle, thereby making its height seem more normal for sitting. Having concluded this would make the wall more useable without compromising its defensive aspect, I became worried that some thrifty bureaucrat looking to reduce costs, as frequently happens, might blue-pencil the footrest out of the design. To prevent this I labeled it as a curb, and when presenting to the National Park Service and various regulatory commissions explained it was there to protect the wall and integral lighting from snowplows and maintenance vehicles. Like the marble benches on the plaza above, the walls and curb have been used continuously by the public ever since.

The benches for Columbus Circle took a different direction. Partly for reasons of climate and comfort, partly for budget concerns, and partly as a nod to other benches throughout the city (designed by Olmsted, Moses, and ourselves), I decided to use wood instead of stone. In Wagner Park, the long wooden slats of ipe had been straight and evocative of docks and boat decks. These benches, however, needed to be curved, not straight. Concerned that there might be serious technical problems with creating parallel curved slats from the dense tropical hardwood we needed to use, we decided to make the benches with short wooden slats spanning the width of the seat and oriented radially. These could then be carved into a gently convex, cushionlike profile, unified and faced with a continuous solid nosing.

As at Wagner Park and the Washington Monument, we emphasized their width to allow people to be able to sit back to back while facing in opposite directions without disturbing each other. Here, too, it seemed wrong to add backs, no matter how useful they might be, because vertical elements would break up the space and make it feel smaller and more confining, too much like a corral. Backs on these benches would also have prevented people from seeing the water in the opposite basins as they looked across the circle, whether seated or standing.

Unlike our benches at Battery Park City or those at the Washington Monument, it didn't seem right to have these seats supported on stone: we wanted them to be lighter and to float above the pavement. So—in the tradition of many wood benches but in a far less obtrusive manner—we settled upon holding them up with metal. Next, in an effort to make this small urban piazza attractive and comfortable at night, our lighting consultant, Hervé Descottes, suggested adding light under the benches, thereby turning them into lampshades and reinforcing the impression that they are floating. This effect, combined with the pale blue of the light, gives the plaza a gay and festive air. People use these benches in every way imaginable, sitting in all directions and positions.

Soon after they were installed, an employee of the New York City Parks and Recreation Department told us that she had received a complaint about them. A representative of the Mayor's office, upon seeing the broad and continuous expanse of the benches, had expressed concern about homeless people sleeping there, and had requested that we design arm rests to prevent such a possibility.

This sort of knuckleheaded bureaucratic vandalism has been the bane of civic space for the past several decades in America. I was opposed to armrests both aesthetically and socially: they were totally antithetical to the entire concept of the benches and would destroy their lines, their appeal, and their flexible use. Somehow I had to show how wrongheaded it was, but I also needed to come up with a proposal that, if it were selected, would make a political statement about what I deemed a misapplication of authority.

I told the Parks Department that we would study the situation and produce a mock-up.

Working with an associate, I decided upon a particular shape in wood that could be fitted onto the recently installed benches. We fabricated a full-size sample out of ipe and took it along to a meeting at the Parks Department headquarters in the Armory on Fifth Avenue, where I set it down on a table. The addition was about two feet long, level in the middle, and pointed at each end, where it rose up slightly in a partial curve. I explained how there would be dozens of these items spaced along the broad benches, radiating from the central monument with its statue of Columbus. As everyone gazed at the model, one of the Park Department officials suddenly blurted out, "My God, they're canoes!" I grinned and said, "Well, they do sort of resemble canoes, now that you mention it."

Some of the attendees laughed and others scowled. For a number of years, the monument had been the site of protest rallies by American Indians on Columbus Day. I was proposing to surround the statue with what appeared to be a ring of native canoes aimed at it silently: a provocative gesture if ever there was one. After the park officials told me that there was no way they would ever allow such a thing, the meeting disintegrated. I never heard about armrests for the Columbus Circle benches again.

Variety Surrounds Me

The world, both natural and human, is stuffed with variety. Igor Stravinsky pointed this out in one of his Norton lectures at Harvard, and succinctly stated his response to this problem in the creation of his music:

> Variety surrounds me on every hand. So I need not fear that I will be lacking in it, since I am constantly confronted by it. Contrast is everywhere. One has only to take note of it. Similarity is hidden. It must be sought out, and is found only after the most exhaustive efforts. When variety tempts me I am uneasy about the facile solutions it offers me. Similarity on the other hand poses more difficult problems, but it offers results that are more solid and hence more valuable to me.[42]

Although I tend to think of this tension as one between "contrast" and "harmony" rather than "variety" and "similarity," I often refer to Stravinsky's observation in discussions with colleagues and students because it is a central consideration in the composition of public spaces, parks, and gardens. One of the principal issues in their design is how to achieve an overall structure where the parts cohere and harmonize with one another in an effective manner while also allowing particular portions or elements to stand out. Variety is easy—almost too easy—to achieve, whereas uniting disparate elements without becoming dull takes effort. And seating in these spaces is often a part of the mixture of elements.

One place that exemplifies an effort to produce a harmonious whole while creating and maintaining variety in its parts is the National Gallery of Art Sculpture Garden, in Washington, DC. The location designated for the garden was just west of the National Gallery of Art and between Constitution Avenue and the National Mall. When we began work there, in 1993, the site contained only a few elements: a large broken circular basin and ring of trees, an obtrusive metal concession building, and a couple of additional trees scattered here and there. We were given no suggestions as to how the site should serve as an exhibition space, nor was there a collection at that time to base a design upon. We decided to create a set of outdoor gallery spaces, or "rooms," of various sizes and shapes around the central basin.

Anticipating large numbers of visitors in all seasons, we knew that seating would be necessary, but where, how much, and what sort was up in the air as well. My instinct was that it should be omnipresent, unobtrusive so as to not interfere with the works of art, and adapted to whichever location or space it was in. Paradoxically, this meant that our final design—if one counted the moveable café chairs and some low planter-seat walls—included

OPPOSITE The basin coping at the National Gallery of Art Sculpture Garden was purposely designed in the form of a seat cushion to provide a place for people to sit and cool their feet on a hot summer day in Washington, DC. Sahar Coston-Hardy photo, OLIN

---

42.   Igor Stravinsky, *Poetics of Music in the Form of Six Lessons* (*Charles Eliot Norton Lectures*), Harvard University Press, revised ed. 1993; second lecture, pp. 31-33.

no fewer than five different types of seating. And yet, far from being visually chaotic, each type was specifically created to harmonize with its particular setting; in fact, one can rarely see two types at the same time.

Two block-long linear spaces served as transition spaces into the garden—one from Constitution and Pennsylvania Avenues to the north and the other from the National Mall to the south. For the long, arcing paths through these spaces I decided on benches that had been designed by Sasaki, Dawson and DeMay for the redevelopment of Pennsylvania Avenue in the early 1970s. This was in part a collegial gesture and in part to situate this new garden in its context—rather like my use of historic benches for the first phase of the esplanade at Battery Park City to ground it in the larger metropolis. To my surprise, the Sasaki benches were no longer manufactured, but this didn't make them less of a good idea; we drew what seemed to be a reasonable reproduction and had them fabricated anew.

For the remainder of the seating in the sculpture garden, however, we returned to the use of stone. As with the Sasaki benches, harmony and similarity were a consideration. The site was surrounded by monumental structures of neoclassical design. Two of them—the National Archive building across Constitution Avenue and the National Gallery of Art across Seventh Street—were designed by John Russell Pope, one of America's most skilled Beaux Arts architects of the early 20th century. Their combined vocabulary of marble curbs, steps, ledges, walls, cornices, and piers comprised the context for the new sculpture garden. Second, a central feature of the garden was to be the reconstruction of a large, circular basin of water, and I'd determined that its coping should be of marble as well.

Almost immediately it seemed obvious that we should make the coping of the basin a good place to sit, and that there should be additional seating continuously around the basin with a generous walkway in between. After a series of quick sketches and studies, each of these circular bands of seating developed a distinct character.

It is often desirable to reduce the height of a coping and its reflection because, when viewed from across the basin, the twinned shadow makes the water level appear lower than it really is. While puzzling over this problem, I recalled a profile used by André Le Nôtre for one of the basins at the Tuileries in Paris that I'd sketched some time before. It began with a generous billowing cushion shape on the outside but then curved down in a concave manner as it approached the water; in essence it was the profile of a scroll, rotated around the circumference of the basin. Setting the outside height at the top of the curve at eighteen inches would produce a comfortable sitting height; the deep reveal beneath would provide a place to tuck one's heels. Inside the basin, we set a weir to function as a continuous drain around the circumference, so that the water level could rise almost to the basin's lip.

Not only do people like to sit around the outside of the pool on the coping, they have learned that in summer, when it's hot, they can sit or recline comfortably on this cushion shape with their feet outstretched in the cooling water; the hundreds of people who do so are proof that this strategy worked out as planned. It also pleases me when something solves more than one problem without calling attention to its multitasking—in this case, a bold basin rim and seat wall that works in two directions, especially seasonally.

The unusual benches we developed to run around the basin's perimeter are variations of the wall-and-slab motif. (By this I mean the motif of putting a bench up against a wall facing out into a space, similar to the example of Seicento benches and ledges worked into the base of an urban palace.) But it seemed stiff and redundant to make them continuously parallel to the rim of the pool. Breaking a circumscribed arc around the basin into segments was the first step.

There were access points to the central basin at each of the cardinal directions—north, east, south, and west—dividing a circumferential walk into quadrants. We then subdivided each of these arcs into five segments to form a set of repetitive sculptural benches. Next came the notion of treating each segment as a shallow crescent—both in plan and in elevation. Studying this, I realized two things. First, that a shallow arc in plan could produce a seat of varying depth.

I'd pondered for years what to do about the fact that people come in different sizes and that their legs (particularly their thighs and shins) are different lengths. What is comfortable for one person is too deep or tall for another, or the reverse; men tend to be bigger than women or children, and so on. We often address such differences indoors with cushions behind the small of the back to make a sofa or chair more comfortable. But employing a shallow arc at the rear of the bench—rather than making it parallel to the front—would create a variable depth: broader in the middle, narrower at the two ends.

Second, I realized that I could vary the height of the back as well, having it start lower at the end, where the seat is the narrowest, sweep gently up to be taller at the bench's center, where the seat is deepest, and then let it descend again, thereby creating a seat and back roughly proportional in each location for tall or small people. This produced a series of banquettes in a shallow scallop plan-form. Both the seat and the back of the bench tilted slightly back in the traditional manner, for comfort, with a slight gap between them for rainwater to drain through; this made them useable almost immediately following a storm or shower and not subject to the freezing and thawing of ice in winter. They were supported simply on tapered stone bases that allowed water to reach drains underneath, keeping the area underfoot at the front of the bench open and dry.

LAURIE OLIN

We then made several studies to consider their silhouette as seen from across the pool, and quickly settled upon a compound curve with a long pedigree. I selected it for its rise and fall, its movement and grace, and its repetitive echo of waves. (It was also a tongue-in-cheek reference to all the neoclassical pretense and achievement in the nearby environment, especially the numerous domes, several of which could be seen from the spot.) Just as with all of our seating, we drew full-size profiles and cross-sections, then made full-size mock-ups of cardboard and foam-core so that men and women in our studio could test them out the best way: by sitting on them. After the necessary adjustments were made, we went into final drawings.

When I presented the sculpture garden design to the US Commission of Fine Arts, Carter Brown, its chairman at the time—who had initiated plans to create the garden when he was Director of the National Gallery—was troubled by the design of these benches. He remarked that their "Chippendale" profile was more suited to domestic-scale furniture and interior use, implying that they were too reminiscent of priceless antiques and seemed too visually active for the situation. In other words, they were surprising in a way that made them stand out: an example of variety rather than similarity.

But of course these tensions play out in complex ways, both in time and in space. I respectfully pointed out that what was later seen as a furniture motif in Colonial highboys had originated as a motif in stone and had been used at *all* scales, indoors and out. It could be found in the façades and stairways of numerous baroque structures designed by Borromini, Bernini, and Guarini in Italy, and later in Balthasar Neumann's rococo pilgrimage churches in Bavaria and southern Germany. In addition, there would be not one bench but twenty in all, and when taken together they would form a coherent and consistent spatial enclosure around the basin, thereby embodying Stravinsky's principle. In any case, I assured him that we would study it carefully. We did, and I concluded that they needed to be the proportion we'd drawn and that the continuous movement of them around the circle was a plus. It wasn't mentioned again. The scheme was approved and we moved on to the challenge of having them fabricated.

To match the stone of the adjacent gallery building by John Russell Pope we had to search about in Tennessee and reopen several quarries that had been closed after I. M. Pei's East Wing was completed. One problem was that at the time no one in the US could mechanically fabricate curves in stone in two directions as we had specified; special milling machines capable of parametric carving had to be obtained from Italy to do the job. The last step of production was to finish the copings and benches by hand—as has been the case for centuries.

The potential for a linear margin or seat wall to metamorphose into other forms and functions has been a topic of interest for some time in our office.

Following the Washington Monument experiment, one of my partners, Cindy Sanders, transformed crash barriers for the Museum of Jewish Heritage in New York into fountains and benches; like those at Columbus Circle, the benches also become light fixtures at night, illuminating the sidewalk and plaza.

Encouraged by such developments, partners Susan Weiler and Richard Roark pushed this notion even further in recent projects at Johns Hopkins Medical Center in Baltimore and Dilworth Park at Philadelphia's City Hall. Both are important but quite different public spaces. The area outside the medical center is quite intimate, intended to allow families, patients, and medical staff to be outdoors for therapeutic reasons; the other is a celebratory civic plaza intended for massive crowds as well as individuals of all manner and mood. For each of these spaces they produced an exercise in plasticity, form, and stone carving that is also practical and functional. At Dilworth Park, the stone used for paving and walls metamorphoses, lifting and shifting into a number of unusual yet well-placed seat walls and benches. The variable dimensions of the seating once again accommodate people of different sizes, shapes, and temperaments, whether convivial or solitary.

For Canal Park in Washington, DC, a former partner, David Rubin, authored several remarkably versatile benches of wood on metal supports which, like those at Hopkins and Dilworth, rise and fall from the pavement in a series of undulating waves, offering privileged places from which to watch children play in an interactive fountain in summer and ice skaters glide by in winter. These benches are just as useful as traditional park benches but also unusual objects in themselves. Both attention-getting and purposefully amusing, they signal to visitors that this is a place of play and lighthearted neighborhood recreation.

Two other examples of such exceptions to the norm by people whose work has been consistently innovative can be found in New York City and Manchester, England, respectively. One is at the stunning High Line, where James Corner (with Lisa Switkin and others) of Field Operations, along with the architects Diller Scofidio + Renfro, has created an extremely popular group of oversized wooden chaise lounge chairs. Unlike such furniture found at resorts and poolsides, which is usually adjustable and made of softer, lighter material, these are made of stacked planks of ipe on metal frames with their backs fixed in a permanent semi-reclining angle. What can be adjusted, however, is their location. These rather hefty broad seats (they are wide enough for two, albeit cozily, which is part of their attraction) are supported on steel wheels that are set on a pair of the former railroad tracks. They can be moved back and forth sideways, allowing a group of people to gang them together or individuals to pull them apart, creating separation and territorial privacy even while being immediately adjacent to a heavily trafficked promenade. This ensemble of handsome, sturdy, and flexible furniture has also been cunningly placed upon a portion of the promenade that faces southwest through an opening in the mass of buildings—a perfect orientation for sunbathing in the late afternoon—and has become enormously popular with both New Yorkers and visitors.

The other example dates from a few years prior to the High Line, when Martha Schwartz experimented with somewhat similar benches in a large public square in Manchester, England. Placing brightly colored level seats on bogies (the pairs of wheel assemblies used at each end of railroad cars), she then set out a flock of these seats on a series of rail tracks arrayed across the paved square. Attractive and whimsical, they also evoke memories of the city's industrial history while creating a unique character for the place without being grim or nostalgic.

Something that is constantly readdressed in the design of all seating is the relationship between the surface of the ground and the surface of the seat—the one structure suspended somehow above the other—while simultaneously questioning whether the two surfaces really need to be two things or instead only different aspects of the same object. It has been pointed out that the most significant feature of Marcel Breuer's early furniture designs while at the Bauhaus in Weimar and Dessau in the early 1930s was that his chairs appeared to "float." There was a lightness that belied their actual structure and weight, so that people sitting on his tubular structures appeared to be suspended in space. [43]

A desire to find fresh expression for whatever support is put in the space between the ground and the seat has been explored in several recent projects by colleagues and former students of mine from the University of Pennsylvania. Highly prominent examples can be seen at the award-winning National 9/11 Pentagon Memorial in Arlington, Virginia, designed by Julie Beckman and Keith Kaseman, and at the High Line project mentioned above, in Manhattan. Both of these projects explore the design expression of benches that literally lift up out of the ground (or deck) to form seating as a displaced portion of that surface. The effect is both surprising and unexpected without being too jarring, because the benches and the surface beneath them are made of the same material; they assert themselves and knit themselves into their surroundings simultaneously.

Critical to the realization of these well-known projects has been the development of computer programs and algorithms that allow parametric modeling of shapes, which can then be developed, documented, and transmitted digitally to the machines of stone-cutters or fabricators. Subtle and complex geometries once explained in freehand sketches and full-size

43.   Barry Bergdoll, "Marcel Breuer, Bauhaus Tradition, Brutalist Invention," *Metropolitan Museum of Art Bulletin*, Summer 2016, p 7.

technical drawings for highly skilled craftsmen to painstakingly carve stone by hand to a large degree have been supplanted by computer modeling that originated within the aerospace industry.

This recent use of parametric modeling has allowed a new baroque, or even rococo, age to flourish in architecture, at least in terms of structural form and the manipulation of metal, stone, or wood. One well-publicized example of this is a large array of benches and seats in a variety of quasi-organic shapes by Chris Reed and his firm Stoss that now whimsically populate the once-barren highway overpass at Harvard University between the Yard and José Luis Sert's Science Center. Made of a sequence of wooden slices, they shift in form from that of benches to chaise lounges to chairs, and even to shapes recalling hospital beds and therapeutic devices.

Like the seating in Canal Park, when unoccupied they register almost as sculpture. On a rainy winter's day, for example, they call to mind a beach scattered with whales, walruses, and seals. But these playful forms are also appealing to students, who slouch about on them in all manner of semi-recline and collapse while studying or socializing. In the balmy weather of spring or fall, when these benches form a series of ledges and seats that are perpetually occupied, they are more like a sea-isle covered with perching birds.

This is only one of many recent experiments by landscape architects all over the world who have realized the importance of public seating and the stimulus to be derived from both taking it seriously and viewing it as an opportunity for invention. At its best, this spirit of experimentation

Resembling great stone cushions or pillows, the benches at the Washington Monument are seen here during installation. Allan Spulecki photo, OLIN

encourages conviviality in our public realm; at its worst, it has led to some pretty dreadful and amateurish new products and fixtures that are willful and dysfunctional. Perhaps the most basic test for civic purpose and its success, whether for a chair or a park, is not how it reads visually but how people interact with the space and make it their own.

The urge to simplify and unite things, to reduce the number of objects cluttering up public space, has occasionally led to interesting developments that involve seating. One example is that of Antoni Gaudí, renowned for his highly original sculptural architecture with its phantasmagoric forms and imagery, who applied his imagination to the design of one of the principal boulevards in Barcelona, the Passeig de Gràcia, and its furnishing. He developed a scheme that combined pedestrian lighting, vehicular lighting, public seating, and street signs all into a singular remarkable fixture, which is then arrayed repetitively along the length of the street. An amalgam of concrete, glazed tile, elaborately wrought metal, and glass, the result is intensely particular—like nothing anywhere else in the universe—and yet also pleasing in its unity.

Several principles are at work in most successful contemporary public landscape projects. First is that too much furniture in the form of separate objects can seem like clutter. (Although intended to be useful, the now all-too-familiar combination of trash and recycling cans, signs, poles, railings, benches, tables, and chairs that one encounters everywhere presents a discordant jumble that ends up making places appear crowded and unattractive instead.) Second, although these projects may be schematically unorthodox or contain elements that are visually arresting, their underlying logic is often deeply familiar.

Toward the end of the twentieth century, many of my peers—architects, landscape architects, and artists who shared my dissatisfaction with the status quo of planning and design in the 1950s, 60s, and 70s—began experimenting with the design of plazas, parks, and the full gamut of their furnishing. Noteworthy work included Parc de la Villette by Bernard Tschumi; Parc André Citroën by Gilles Clément, Allain Provost, and Patrick Berger; the Jardin Atlantique by Brun, Pena, and Schnitzler; and other urban spaces that followed in the wake of the *Grand Projets* of d'Estaing, Mitterrand, and Chirac. In the Netherlands, leaders of this wave of fresh urban landscape design included Adriaan Geuze, Jerry van Eyck, and others of the firm West 8.

Each of the new French parks produced fresh imagery and different-looking furniture; less discussed was that they also maintained traditional attributes—the inhabited edge, overlooks, seating beneath trees and arbors, and urban theater. Their success was as much a result of their provision of familiar functional tropes as it was due to their visual novelty. People still sat about watching each other, socializing and relaxing, reading and napping, albeit on new and at times odd-looking but interesting objects, decks, chairs, and benches made of familiar or unexpected materials. The formal and visual novelties, in other words, were undergirded by experiential similarities.

In much the same way, West 8's early central square redesign for Rotterdam, despite its stunning appearance, actually functioned like a traditional Italian piazza, offering continuous linear seating facing what amounts to a performance space. While a series of tall adjustable overhead lamps suggestive of giant mechanical insects stalk the length of the square, attracting attention, the seating couldn't be more ordinary and quietly effective. Like the more recent American experiments discussed above, these are merely examples of finding new ways to do an old thing: namely, making places for large numbers of people, often strangers to one another, to sit together comfortably, often under trees or facing a water feature, while simultaneously creating a sense of unique character for each place.

If one strong motive for my own decades-long exploration of built-in furniture has been a desire to develop spaces that do not present cacophony, another has been an urge to be inviting: to make things more ample or plentiful than they probably need to be. All too often, benches set out by agencies and property owners are of the six-feet-long variety: they're cheaper than those eight feet long, but as noted earlier this means that fewer people can use them. Knowing that the longer a bench becomes the more strangers it can accommodate, and that people frequently wish to sit without feeling compelled to interact, we have made some of ours twenty feet long or longer. People populate them and produce a de facto community of strangers, which is a civic benefit, but one that is not coerced. This is related to what Lawrence Halprin and others have referred to as design that is "open score" as opposed to "closed score"– in other words, design that allows choice rather than delimiting it or proscribing certain activities and only allowing particular others.

Thinking again about Stravinsky's remark about contrast and similarity, it is interesting to reflect upon how the fundamental freedom, pleasure, and comfort of moveable chairs presents a dramatic foil to fixed benches, ledges and walls, but also how well they tend to work in combination with each other. It can be seen in many a café and restaurant. I first consciously realized this in the cafés and coffeehouses of Vienna with their banquettes, tables, and chairs. I realized that this was also a feature of American diners and bar-and-grill establishments that I'd known as a youth. Chairs are almost always lighter in appearance and mass than traditional wood benches and don't appear to fill plazas and spaces as much, thereby not blocking movement and sight. However, they don't really shape or define space (except for quite small or intimate groups) in the manner that is possible using larger, more opaque, fixed seat walls and extended benches.

As it turns out, unlike the fixed seating arrangements of industrial chairs and tables argued against earlier, the extended benches and ledges we have experimented with attract people. This is for several reasons. First, *they are used to frame and shape space, not merely occupy it.* This automatically puts people in the position of being safe observers overlooking a scene from a perimeter and not being "on stage'" until they choose to be so by moving into the space and view of others. It's the favorite place to sit in every culture.

In this regard benches, like chairs, engender different uses and behavior, civic being only one. Michael Jakob in a recent essay suggests three possible salient roles they might take: *scopic,* wherein one employs a bench to learn how to view something; *sociopolitical,* when the bench assists one in deciphering and responding to the structure and forces embodied in public, private, or mixed spaces; and finally *transcendental,* whereby in using a particular bench one learns how to understand oneself.[44]

The first mode, widely used in 18th-century gardens, positioned one to receive references and allusions to travel, literature, and philosophy. The second seems well demonstrated in the benches of the piazzas and palazzos of Renaissance Italy and in classical antiquity, as mentioned above. Jakob's last suggestion seems perhaps idealistic, except for the potential of self realization and reflection that can be obtained simply by being (sitting) alone outdoors, stimulated by the surrounding environment, awake and aware of one's place in the world, physically and mentally.

In all of this I would like to call attention to the relationship between the two words "situate" and "sitting"; as one takes one's fixed spot in the landscape, one also becomes *of* it, situated within a larger context.

---

44.   Michael Jakob, op. Cit., p. 24.

In addition to their usual role, the benches at Columbus Circle in
Manhattan also function as a decorative light source for visitors in the
evening. Moving the water of the fountain from the monument to the
perimeter allowed people to utilize the memorial base for additional
seating with a back. Laurie Olin photo, OLIN

LAURIE OLIN

Ordinariness and Form

One fundamental aspect of the numerous benches we have designed and built is a great concern for dimension and proportion. Another is the choice of the material and its treatment. The concept of "no ideas but in things"[45] that one encounters in the poetry of Ezra Pound, William Carlos Williams, and Wallace Stevens is central to both Zen Buddhism and modern Western art. These poets didn't believe, of course, that there are to be no ideas in art, but rather that works of art should "be" rather than "tell." Ideas were to be conveyed directly through the medium, whether poetry, painting, music, or architecture, not through talking about them.

Like Whitman earlier, Williams presented everyday material from the world readily at hand around him: the weeds in the ditch beside the road, the white chickens in his backyard, the chilled plums in the icebox. He openly declared quotidian experience a worthy subject for art and our consideration. At the same time, he worked carefully on how to fashion his material on the page, striving to produce a rhythm and texture he detected in the English language as it was spoken by his fellow Americans.

In both art and architecture, there was a deep interest in the relationship between materials and the production of ideas. Painters like Pablo Picasso, Clyfford Still, and others frequently chose to let the canvas itself become a participant in the composition and surface of a finished piece, while architects like Louis Kahn, Marcel Breuer, and Tadao Ando carefully presented the marks of the making in their work: the joints, the arrangement of the holes left from snap ties, or the texture of boards in the forms that shaped their concrete structures. These elements functioned as both traces of the labor and an essential part of the merit of the work itself.

One of my instructors once told me about a moment when the painter Edgar Degas was frustrated that, despite having lots of ideas, his attempts to write poetry were unsuccessful, and how Paul Valéry told him, "My dear Degas, poems are made from words, not ideas." The annals of art are filled with anecdotes to this effect. The highly influential architect and one-time director of the Bauhaus, Ludwig Mies van der Rohe, is famously reported to have once said, "God is in the details." Very few real designers would disagree. It is one thing to have an idea and another altogether to give it effective and convincing form. How one makes something and gives it expression is as important as its concept—in landscape architecture as in any art. One of the finest modern landscape architects, Dan Kiley, once turned to me and declared, "Proportion is everything!"

Despite commonplace rules of thumb about seat height and depth, we keep starting afresh. This may sound silly; why do it again if you have done it

45.   William Carlos Williams, "Paterson," "Spring and All," "The Red Wheelbarrow," and "This is Just to Say," *The Collected Earlier Poems*, p. 233, p. 241, p. 277, p. 354; New Directions, 1951.

OPPOSITE PAGE Visitors utilizing the curving benches on the terrace of the Washington Monument, Washington, DC. Peter Mauss/Esto photo, OLIN

before? The answer is that more than one thing can be comfortable, and there are different combinations that turn out to work. Time after time, in order to produce yet another version of comfortable seating for a new and particular place, I have built full-size mock-ups of benches that are in design and asked staff members of different sizes, shapes, and genders to sit on them.

From both numerous studies and personal experiment I've concluded that seats can be comfortable in a range of heights from fourteen to eighteen inches, depending upon the angles of the seat and the back and their relation to each other. While it is tempting to say there are no rules, there are definitely things that seem universally uncomfortable or wrong having to do with being too high or too low. Twelve inches above the ground is almost always too low; thus when we sit on steps we often extend our legs and feet beyond the next immediate step from our perch or we find our knees up near our chest. Likewise, twenty inches or more in height usually results in having to stretch or hoist oneself up to that level, only to have one's feet dangle awkwardly in the air as a small child's do, a condition of insecurity few people enjoy.

It's elementary knowledge that the angle of a seat back has a great deal to do with comfort. This leads to the consideration of both the purpose of the seat and the sort of behavior that is to be desired or encouraged in the sitter at the site under design. Given the sinuousness of most human spines, truly vertical backs are not only stiff but also uncomfortable. Among the most uncomfortable seats in history have been the many straight-backed benches, pews, and chairs placed in Christian churches and cathedrals through the centuries that are intended to make one sit up and pay attention rather than relax into a private drowse or reverie. If, however, the intent is to promote leisure, longer-term stays, even sunbathing or napping, then a back that tilts back at an angle resembling a poolside chaise lounge is appropriate. For example, it is impossible to sit erect in the sort of folding canvas sling chairs commonly found in English parks and resorts. Like hammocks, they enforce a semi-reclining posture. If, on the other hand, it is preferable that visitors don't camp out for long durations but instead remain a brief time and move on, allowing others to do the same, then something more vertical while still reasonably comfortable—less like an easy chair and a bit more like an office chair—is in order.

Seats that are too deep can be uncomfortable because a person can't put her feet on the ground and have the support of the back. With interior furniture this is often resolved by the introduction of cushions, which are seen as decorative as well, a phenomenon that has led to the production of innumerable deep sofas and living-space seats that emphasize comfort and lounging about in a semi-reclining manner. This has not been very common or seen as practical in most outdoor public seating.

For this reason I was somewhat surprised on first going to Syntagma Square in Athens to find it furnished with rows of what in America are called "easy chairs": wide efforts with broad arms and thick stuffed cushions covered with outdoor canvas, plastic, or leatherette for the seats and backs. Some were of such ample width that they verged upon becoming settees, and once a visitor settled into these seats, it took some effort to rise out of them again. The design of this seating explicitly stated that a large number of Athenians were expected to come to this park and hang out for lengthy periods—perhaps most of the day. Their implied leisure and comfort made public squares in other countries, even Mediterranean ones, seem positively puritanical. In America, upholstered outdoor furniture used to be limited to private gardens and resorts. In the last decade, however, it has become more common in public—especially in cafés and a new generation of beer gardens—but still not in civic spaces. (One needn't go to such extremes, however; one can provide for a reasonable degree of comfort using stone, wood, or metal.)

Several decades ago the industrial designer Henry Dreyfuss and a protégé, Niels Diffrient, performed exhaustive research on human dimensions, proportions, and comfort for the US Government and private industry, developing some of the most effective ergonometric equipment, guidelines, and furniture in history. It would be a mistake, however, to say, "that's it, these are the rules," as seems to have been the conclusion of the study recently employed by airlines noted above. This is because of the variable motives and moods intended for public seating.

One critical distinction is the difference between seating that is indoors and seating that is outside. We may be the same animals in both places, but how we move, how we perceive our situation, and what we feel is different. Stairs that feel normal indoors are terribly wrong outdoors—something that a great number of architects still seem not to grasp. Outdoors one strides more than indoors; in the former case, the ratio of vertical rise to horizontal run of a stair needs to produce a much flatter angle of climb.[46] So, too, there is a need for amplitude and a change in scale outdoors simply because there is more space—the eye sees farther, and one's sense of territory and perception expands. Things that seem large and bold indoors can appear small, insignificant, even fragile when taken outdoors. This is one reason, as I often say to my students and colleagues, it is always better to err on the side of generosity. We, too, often feel insignificant in the public realm; gestures and accommodations that help to counteract this are therefore all the more valuable.

Another basic consideration is that different materials are often best fashioned in different ways. The fact that this principle is frequently ignored remains one of the mysteries of architectural education today. How different

---

46.   I remember a lovely and witty essay on this topic by James Marston Fitch published sometime in the 1970s that I have been unable to locate, unfortunately. Somebody should find and reprint it.

LAURIE OLIN

substances are cut, shaped, bent, or fastened has an effect upon the relationship and angles of seat and back, joinery, and even the dimensions. If it were easy or always the same, there would be no reason for so many furniture manufacturers, designers, and their products to exist. This goes beyond mere accommodation or style. Chippendale, Sheraton, Hepplewhite, Stickley, Mies, and Aalto all made superb furniture, and all solved basic problems. Each produced furniture that invariably expressed their time and personality, and the products of each of these designers look and feel very different from the others.

Our office has never attempted to create any particular imagery nor affect a house style; Bob Hanna even went so far as to write in one of our early brochures that we do not seek "art for art's sake" in our work. I didn't believe that to be true in all instances, and we finally quarreled on this point, but certainly none of my partners or I set out to make furnishings that are strident or call attention to themselves. One habit, though, has been to play with the normal scale or proportion of one or more elements in our design of benches and seats so as to make a common thing special in some way. Frequently I've stretched things, making benches longer and more generous than is usual or expected—or, possibly, needed—for the sheer pleasure of it.

At Dilworth Park in Philadelphia a number of broad stone benches become transformed into planter walls and, eventually, into curbs. Laurie Olin photo, OLIN

Despite my love for stone, like other designers all over, I have made many benches from wood. Benches around the world are fashioned from wood for several reasons. First, wood is cheaper to harvest and shape than stone or metal. It is also a warmer, softer material, and more comfortable to sit upon when the weather is very hot or cold. A fundamental characteristic of wood, however, is that it tends to be available only in fairly long straight pieces because today much of it comes from trees commonly grown in plantations that produce tall, thin specimens for harvest. With the disappearance of the majority of old-stand trees on many continents, large dimensions of clear wood have become scarce and costly. If one wants to work with anything other than thin sheets, sticks, or strips, one must somehow glue or fasten pieces together. Then, in order to create nonlinear shapes or curved forms or surfaces, the wood has to be bent or laminated into volumes thick enough to be carved by CNC milling machines, or arranged on some sort of armature that provides the form desired. Even then, portions such as endpieces, nosings, and edges are often carved from larger planks or logs.

In our first wooden benches with nonstandard dimensions, we worked with straight pieces held together by a metal subframe in a variation of 19th-century practice. Earlier I noted that I'd made the benches at Columbus Circle from short pieces of wood arranged radially because I didn't believe that a tropical hardwood such as ipe could be bent effectively in uniformly spaced parallel strips. To my delight and astonishment, while working with ZGF architects several years later in Portland, Oregon—a region known for its wood products and expertise in making boats (which subsequently led to producing early airplane frames)—we were fortunate to collaborate with a woodworker who did indeed find a way to bend this dense wood into strips for some curving benches at Director Park. As at Columbus Circle, people can sit on these benches facing in either direction, and as at the National Gallery's Sculpture Garden, people can put their feet in the water if they sit on the concave side facing the basin, or, conversely, they can sit on the convex side with their backs to the fountain and have their feet on dry pavement.

The large semicircular bench at Director Park also takes advantage of topography in an odd fashion. One of the dilemmas facing designers often is that most of the world is not flat, and paths in parks often slope one way or another. Placing benches along them is common, but if the path slopes a great deal there is a question of whether the seat should be level or parallel to the slope. When a number of traditional six- or eight-foot-long benches step down a slope, it often looks peculiar. Yet if one makes the benches parallel to the slope, they may feel odd to sit on, depending upon their tilt.

The situation becomes more troubling if one wants a long bench or seat wall while desiring a nice level top. In Portland the plaza was sloping steeply—nearly at five percent, which is the steepest slope acceptable for a handicap-accessible ramp. Realizing I could make a semicircular dam or weir to catch water for a basin on this slope, I simply put a generous curved-wood top on it. The resulting seat is set level, but the ground slopes away and then back up. This has the odd result that, at the uphill ends, the bench appears to be lying on the ground like a big wooden cushion but then gradually becomes elevated as the pavement slopes away downhill until, at the center of the curve, it is just under two feet high. Only in two brief spots is it ever the conventional eighteen inches high. This gradient of heights and comfort appeals to many, especially children. There is a curious friendliness to this bench, as it seems somehow like some sort of big, soft, sleeping creature.

While such developments can be welcome, one must be careful that variations from the expected don't produce something that is wasteful or grotesque rather than surprising and pleasing. People expect that most outdoor seating will be a variation on chairs or benches (sofas, divans, settees). There are two other fundamental types of seating that I've experimented with from time to time: the hassock, or footstool; and bleacher-type theater seating. Again, as with benches, these have often been accompanied by one sort or another of distortion or transformation in either their size or their proportion.

First the hassock. It is an archaic type, an example of which I ran into on the ancient site of Aphrodisias in Turkey. While wandering around the spectacular ruins in this remote mountain region, at the bottom of a small theater, I happened to come upon a full-size replica of a bronze folding stool, complete with a plump stuffed cushion, carved out of marble. Since this stone stool was clearly an outdoor substitute for a more precious item, I surmised that the cushion it imitated had been made of fine leather or cloth. We don't generally do stools or large hassocks for public spaces. However, there is an exception that my colleagues and I call the *keblis*.

Back in the early 1960s, when a group of Richard Haag's students were working in his office in Seattle, someone suggested making a large square wooden platform for one of his projects that could be used either as seating or as a low table of sorts for potted plants and other things. It was eighteen inches high and about eight feet square, made of Douglas fir two-by-fours. It was supported in such a way that it appeared to float a bit above the ground. It seemed strangely familiar—a neatened-up relative of Huck Finn's raft, maybe—but useful. It was also an inexpensive way to provide a lot of informal public seating for a college campus or a civic space such as the Seattle World's Fair site. Since none of us had seen such an item before, we didn't know what to call it. Ilze Grinbergs (a young architect working in the office of landscape architect Bill Teufel), who later cofounded the prominent Seattle landscape architecture and planning firm Jones and Jones, referred to it as a keblis. When asked what that meant, she said simply that keblis meant "thing" in Latvian. Since then, those who were around Rich's office at the time have used both the device and the name.

In my case, it has come in handy on several occasions when the only way to plant trees on a terrace on a roof deck or over some structure was in a raised planter. Never a fan of trees in raised boxes, I truly hate trees in raised planters. I much prefer to see them come out of the ground or surface of a space, whether it be a paved piazza or turf. This has often been impossible, however, on many late 20th- and early 21st-century sites. A keblis can disguise a planter which, when covered, provides a flexible platform with trees growing through its deck. It can also be used for informal seating; as a plinth for pots and plants; or as a small performance stage or bandstand. The courtyard of the Federal Reserve Bank of Kansas City, the west terrace of the Barnes Foundation in Philadelphia, and the pool at the Hotel Arts on the waterfront in Barcelona all incorporate keblises in interesting ways. They may be unfamiliar, but people quickly realize they are also to sit on.

Theater seating: Some of the oldest seating surviving from antiquity is that of Greek and Roman theaters. Travelers have their favorites, often heavily influenced by the landscape setting. Those familiar with the theaters of Delphi or Pergamon might have a hard time choosing which is the most stunning, but any number of smaller theaters are also quite wonderful. The oldest I've seen personally is probably that of King Minos at Knossos in Crete, which predates those of classical Greece. It consists of two sets of broad rectangular steps set at right angles to each other facing a small stone-paved stage or square. The stage sits at the "head" of a path referred to as a sacred way, a stone street that comes up from the valley below to the hilltop of the palace site. It seems a perfect theater, and also a great example of the sort of urban knuckle or linkage that Bill MacDonald describes in subsequent Roman urbanism. It is simple, as quiet in its elements as the site can be when not swarming with tourists, and could probably accommodate several hundred people standing, as was common for many ceremonies, plays, and events. As in the later stone hillside theaters of the Greeks, the seats are a comfortable height and the trays sufficiently broad to allow for both the legs of those seated and enough room to pass by them.

The grace and curve of the later theaters, the slope of their tiers (sometimes shallow, but more often steep), the strength and solidity of the blocks of stone, the carving of the lip of the seats and their deep shadows, the dual rhythm of the trays of seats and the pathways of stairs carved into them: all come together to form a handsome structure that looks as good empty as it does full (something that one can't say about too many contemporary public gathering spaces). I don't know a landscape architect who doesn't admire these ancient theaters, and who hasn't at some point tried his or her hand at creating theater seating at some scale.

In America, from the late 19th century through the period of the WPA, amphitheaters were created in parks and public sites across the country.[47] Many survive today. One of my favorites is an intimate amphitheater at

---

47.   At the time of writing, Linda Jewell, Professor Emeritus, University of California, Berkeley, is completing a long-awaited book, *Gathering on the Ground: Experiencing Landscape in American Outdoor Theaters*, that documents many of the most iconic as well as lesser-known examples.

Swarthmore College outside Philadelphia. This site is loved by all who know it—in large part because of its forest setting and the fact that a number of trees are incorporated somewhat randomly into its design. These trees, mostly tulip poplars, drift across several tiers of the upper arc of the seats and provide a partial canopy. The theater gives a domesticated quality to the woods while the trees lend a charming rusticity to the theater, along with a strange sense of its being inhabited even when empty.

My other great favorite is the Red Rocks Amphitheatre outside of Denver, Colorado, in the foothills of the front range of the Rocky Mountains. Built in a natural ravine between two massive outlying walls of red sandstone, this theater rivals many of the classical world for drama and landscape setting. It is also remarkably simple in its parts. Its dramatic bowl of ascending seats is filled with curving, low retaining walls of stacked red sandstone from which continuous wooden seats are cantilevered on brackets. Immediately behind each band of these seat walls is a walkway (originally of packed crushed stone and now of concrete). It is stunning in its simplicity and grandeur.

There have been several occasions in my career when I have succumbed to the temptation to create amphitheater seating. The two most successful examples are at Robert Wagner Jr. Park at Battery Park City and at Exchange Square in London. The first has been described somewhat above, and is comprised of stone ledges facing the Hudson River and the Statue of Liberty. The other looks into the great Victorian train shed of Liverpool Street Station. It consists of broad stone ledges, which can be used for public seating, overlooking a small lawn, stone bandstand, and busy public walkway – emphasizing that urban squares can be a form of public theater. We planned the square with a team of architects and engineers. Influenced by the prototypical squares I had studied when young, I made certain that there were a number of active building entries, cafés, a pub, and a wine bar on its perimeter, along with shade from trees. There is also a fountain that cascades down a set of ledges adjacent to a flight of stairs and the terraced seating. The need to provide good access for the disabled suggested a curving ramp, which in turn led me to gather the stone bleacher seats together in a twist, forming a column at one end from which one of the architects hung a canopy over the bandstand. It all faces south: a preferred orientation in northern climes. Like many of my favorite spaces, whether urban squares or ancient theaters, it looks good empty, in the rain, with a handful of people sprinkled about, or packed at lunch when entertainment is supplied on a joyful sunny day. Imagine my pleasure when I happened through the square on a drizzly London day and found several architectural students carefully measuring the stone seats.

The designers of the High Line in New York have had a similar triumph with some bleacher seating that they have set into the first phase of their superb scheme at one of the transition points at which there is a shift in the direction of the walkway—just the sort of place that such design events seem

Social activity can carry over
into winter in public places that
encourage their use in ways that
seem familiar and comfortable, as
here in Director Square, Portland,
Oregon. Laurie Olin photo, OLIN

particularly well suited for. Theirs takes the form of ample wooden steps and broad bleacher seats that look out and down one of the streets in lower Manhattan. Frequently crowded, this seating allows people to turn their back on everyone above as they look out over everyone below them, creating a distinct space between the High Line and the street. People can be seen eating, working on laptops, reading, talking with friends, or simply watching an ongoing stream of the vehicles moving away beneath them, along with pedestrians walking in all different directions. This particular area of seats is a highlight of this public esplanade, one of its special places.

One puzzling phenomenon occurs when things that are intended to comment on something are made from the very stuff they are meant to represent. When, for example, is a chair not a chair? Utility and comfort are important, but they aren't everything; certainly not always. Proof of this can be found in the number of well-known pieces of furniture produced by artists in the late 20th century, which to a degree have had a pronounced if not well-understood effect upon landscape furnishing. Several prominent artists associated with the minimalist movement in American art have built and sold seats and benches of their design, usually through galleries. Certainly as concerned about materials, craft, and form as any architect, they proudly eschew much of the sensibility of the professions with our adherence to safety and functionality. In their insistence that they are making art and therefore it need not be accommodating in the usual sense, the furniture they have produced has generally been simple in the extreme – often a few slabs of wood or stone, cut in precise shapes, frequently dogmatically rectangular, and joined together simply. They are as much diagrams as they are furniture for use.

Donald Judd—perhaps best known for several sets of heroic sculptures in Marfa, Texas, that are universally admired—created many series of boxes in various materials that can be found in contemporary museums around the world. He also produced a number of simple plywood tables and chairs for his own workshop and family. If they weren't so precise and calculated in their measurement and joinery, one might call them simple-minded and crude. There is no obvious attempt to accommodate the human form, or to cater to others. The plywood backs are vertical, the seats horizontal, and the supports vertical. Like his famous boxes, the angles are ninety degrees. For those devoted to his art and career, these pieces are also considered works of art, and highly valued—so much so that they prompted exhibitions, publications, and even reproductions for sale. For many others, though, they are uncomfortable and suspiciously reminiscent of the emperor's new clothes.

Scott Burton also fashioned seats and tables as works of art and installation pieces intended for human use. His most famous works are made of blocks of sharply cut granite, at times with the profile of the anonymous Adirondack chairs that are now marketed by a number of manufacturers.

They usually consist of strong, uncompromising forms, and in the case of several prominent installations (Battery Park City, National Gallery of Art, the Walker Center) are intended for use. His chairs are generally a bit more comfortable to actually sit in than Judd's, but the table seating arrangements are awkward and impractical—in part because of the distance between seat and table and in part because they are manifestly unmovable. Again, they are more of a diagram—the presentation of a representation of ordinary furniture—rather than the thing itself.

Architects who were closely allied to artists in this period began to produce furniture of a basic and somewhat atavistic combination of simple forms and humble materials. Early in his career the most innovative and sculptural architect of recent decades, Frank Gehry, produced a number of chairs and sofas from corrugated cardboard; lumpy and crude-looking, they proved to be strangely comfortable and soft to sit in. Later he furnished his office and clients with simple-seeming furniture—made from slabs and sheets of raw plywood, reminiscent of Judd, or of large chunky timbers with echoes of Carl Andre, but on castors and more accommodating. He also designed a line of furniture for Knoll made from thin strips of wood, inspired in large part by peach baskets.

In the past two decades, an attitude inspired by Arte Povera, Minimalism, and the sculpture of Donald Judd, Richard Serra, Carl Andre, Jackie Ferrara, and Scott Burton has seeped into landscape architecture and public furnishing designed by younger firms on both sides of the Atlantic. Rectangular concrete slabs, cubes, and boxes; logs and large timbers barely cut, shaped, or adjusted; roughly finished cubic wood plinths; stacks like woodpiles; and box-like trestles of slats or lamination have become common. It is difficult to fault an attitude that purposefully seeks to avoid fussiness and eschews fetishizing style in exterior furnishing. Still, there is also an attitude uneasily close to the aesthetic equivalent of anti-intellectualism: either a willful or witless absence of consideration of craft, comfort, and the successes of design history. Some of these pieces even exhibit a sort of "in your face" aggressiveness. While I'm not willing to condemn all of this, a lot of the recent work one encounters in parks and plazas seems a dumbing down of the field by a generation trained very differently than I was, who have other skills and interests. Donald Judd and Frank Gehry these designers are not.

Nature and Change

A subtext of this book about seating has obviously been a concern with the public realm and civic space, but I have not particularly attempted to analyze or fully explain it—that would be a serious undertaking of great difficulty. Some points I can and should make, however. One is that there is much more involved in the design of successful civic space than merely being able to sit about comfortably. Another is that designers and their designs cannot *enforce* sociability. They can defeat civic participation (as Holly Whyte has amply demonstrated), they can restrict or channel movement, and they can prevent sociability through inept or negative design. But design doesn't make people do anything. It can, however, *afford* certain activities—even encourage them—and that possibility is something to be considered and cultivated.

A number of years ago, before it was rebuilt, I presented the Bryant Park plans to a group of academics and interested intellectuals from NYU one evening in Greenwich Village. Among them were the urban historians and critics Carl Schorske and Richard Sennett, whose writings on Vienna and Paris I found provocative and inspiring. Sennett attacked the project and me with an energy that surprised me. He saw the project as a usurpation of a free and open portion of the public realm that accommodated denizens from the margins of society. To him, a powerful elite was converting a democratic shared space into a preserve for the bourgeoisie; it was simply another form of gentrification and displacement of the "have-nots" of society.

I was hurt and put out, in part because I had begun my career of involvement in the public realm with both a study of Seattle's Skid Road residents and a painful but successful fight to save the Pike Place Market, in opposition to prevailing middle-class views and establishment planning attitudes that were seeking to demolish it. Unlike Sennett, I didn't feel that the park was functioning as a "democratic shared space," as so few people felt comfortable using it.

If Sennett portrayed the Bryant Park restoration project as the hijacking of a public park by private interests, I regarded it as taking the park back for the hard-pressed middle class. As mentioned earlier, I felt that the well-to-do had adequate private resources to produce their own salubrious realms, whereas the poor and lower classes would certainly benefit from a safer, healthier, and more beautiful park. In other words, I was openly advocating that a public place carefully created by and for the middle class could benefit all members of society, even the homeless. I still feel that way.

In the twenty-five years since construction ended, certain events and entertainments—Fashion Week, say, or the December holiday market—have taken place there that might bolster Sennett's argument. For most of the year, though, the renovation has been a huge victory in the reclamation

OPPOSITE PAGE The playful, undulating ribbon bench at Canal Park in Washington, DC, sends a clear signal to children and adults alike that they are meant to have fun while also suggesting that there isn't a particularly right or wrong way to use it. Sahar Coston-Hardy photo, OLIN

and reassertion of public space, civic behavior, and community. It is also my belief that a significant aspect of the remarkable success of this park is attributable to the type, quantity, and quality of the seating that is afforded within it: free, variable, moveable, and democratic.

In Western society there can be significant variations in affordance and behavior even within the same country, and this is illustrated by the different ways people sit in public—some of which are intended, and some of which aren't. A classic example of the first category are the curved benches adjacent to a sculpture of Alice in Wonderland in Central Park, which were clearly intended for the use of parents and nannies who bring children to play and climb about on the sculpture. There is an implicit understanding that these benches offer an excellent place to sit comfortably in the sun and oversee the play and safety of the children while also offering community with others of similar life conditions at the moment.

Examples of the second category range from the opportunistic use of random physical elements such as walls, steps, and railings to boxes, cartons, and portions of structures (fountains and buildings) by an infinite number of homeless and indigent individuals. One I recall was the discovery of an elderly woman who for a period of time could be discovered lying asleep in the morning on the rim of one of our basins at Columbus Circle. Later in the day women and small children, despite the proximity nearby of generous benches and the stepped base of the monument, also occasionally use this coping for seating.

A more extreme case of opportunity leading to the encouragement of community behavior can be seen at the Memorial to the Murdered Jews of Europe in Berlin, which I helped Peter Eisenman (and for a time Richard Serra, before he left the project) to realize. Deemed a success by many people as a sobering, even grim, memorial to the millions of people murdered by the Nazi regime, it has also taken its place among the living as a free and open site in the heart of the city.

While the tops of some of the concrete steles (or plinths) are level with the ground and some tower overhead, there are a large number that—their numbing orthogonal order, spacing, and harsh form notwithstanding—provide an opportunity for perching, sitting, and gathering. As a result, people commonly do so—to rest, check their phones, consult a map or guidebook, meet a friend for lunch, or even hold an impromptu class or discussion. Here one can observe the ad hoc development of community that such a place can generate, even with no intentional expression of seating.

This disturbs others and has led to criticism of the memorial—namely, that it affords unanticipated and possibly unintended activity that is not deemed respectful of the dead, rather than remaining a place solely for mourning and reflection. That children can be found playing here does not offend me; instead it reminds me of the school my son attended in

Philadelphia next to the graveyard of a historic church, where games at recess sometimes spilled into the areas between the headstones. I think, in fact, that the unanticipated integration of the memorial into the quotidian life of Berlin is a good thing—humanity rises from its ashes and goes on. In some cultures and places, such an outburst of assembly and conviviality would promptly attract the authorities and be stopped, but in an open and free society the ability to gather spontaneously should be seen as a reassuring event.

One attribute of what we call Nature is that it operates according to certain laws and replicates certain patterns. But another of its fundamental attributes is that Nature is dynamic, not static—and we are part of nature. While there are many problems that may seem constant, the natural world and its processes keep finding fresh ways to adapt to them. So too, it is with people and their creations.

In the summer of 1982 before I began to teach at Harvard I had a long and delightful breakfast with Peter Walker, the outgoing chairman of the Landscape Architecture Department. Pete described his growing involvement with contemporary art and the methods employed by certain sculptors he admired as acts of discovery. He was most interested in what was unique about our moment in time and culture. What separated and distinguished it from those of the past? How might one be able to find expressive form for such differences?

For my part, I mentioned my years of studying the history of landscape architecture, as well as researching particular individuals and great works of design, and how I was interested in understanding which aspects of those works could still be of enormous value, whether technically or culturally. What could be distilled from the past that was timeless? We both appreciated the value of the other's perspective, even to the point of knowing that both skeins of thought were not only complementary but also necessary if we were to achieve the level of our ambitions and become truly successful in our future work. Despite our different points of departure, our work revolved around similar concerns: invention, variety, novelty, continuity, tradition, precedent, and typology.

On the one hand, as cultured beings we crave comfort and need safety. On the other hand, we also desire stimulus, novelty, and delight with all the implications of aesthetics, taste, and surprise. We alternate between wanting the old and familiar, the tried and true, and the new and different, the unknown and fresh. How to revivify old themes and motifs, whether in narrative, poetry, music, painting, or public space, is a fundamental task—an obligation, even—for those in art and design.

Still, it may seem odd or untimely to concern oneself at such length with how poorly or well-designed seating can influence our experience of public space and community at a moment when more and more people seem to be less attentive to their physical surroundings than ever, immersed as they are in both private and public with digital devices, cell phones, and virtual realms rather than the real thing. At the same time, millions of other people around the world today are struggling with matters of individual and family survival, contending with challenges of the most fundamental sort in their surroundings: drought, famine, flooding. In even the most developed regions of the world, many communities are fragmented by political repression, ethnic tensions, and economic disparities. Still, the need for adequate public space remains a constant as we witness the marches, parades, celebrations, memorials, and protests—both organized and unplanned—that are repeatedly enacted in the heart of our cities, great and small.

We have a need as citizens to be able to be physically together: this continues to be a demand of societies everywhere. And notions of place and identity are central to our consideration of those spaces. The way in which we choose to furnish them reveals attitudes regarding community, sociability, local history, and character. It speaks to where we are in the world, and how we know that we are in one place and not another.

The worldwide adoption of blue jeans and mobile phones, of standardized measures, phrases, vehicles, and inexpensive, mass-produced food, combined with the hegemony of a handful of languages, popular music, cinema, and sports, weaponry, and digital media, have led to a widespread loss of regional differences that has been remarked upon by many. The vast tourist industry of our era undermines these differences, even as it depends on them. By several important means of measurement, including public health, this hegemony has benefited hundreds of millions of people around the world. At the same time, many of these same people have experienced a troubling diminishment of invaluable heritage and sense of identity.

There is a widespread pleasure taken by people around the world in having a particular landscape that distinguishes them and is uniquely theirs. Unfortunately, a created civic space—like any other human product—can be placeless, tasteless, and generic, or it can be particular, full of character, and absolutely local. In our era, when so many individuals and nations are striving to find a way to participate in the modern world without losing themselves and their souls, the landscapes we make can not only resist such losses but also generate new possibilities for community. One humble but particularly effective device in this effort is the manner in which we frame and inhabit our public spaces. Strangely enough, one of the keys to that is how, where, and why we sit in them—both alone and together.

OPPOSITE PAGE Few mature public spaces rely upon a single type of seating. At Director Park in Portland, Oregon, one finds long, wall-mounted wood benches with high backs in combination with moveable tables and chairs on a café terrace. Laurie Olin photo, OLIN

Acknowledgements

I am grateful for the generous support and gift of time granted me by the American Academy in Rome and the Guggenheim Foundation that started me on the path documented in this work and to the many clients that have allowed and even encouraged my office and me to experiment; they have been remarkable and are due our grateful thanks. The Philadelphia Athenaeum's Bruce Laverty (Curator of Architecture) and Michael Seneca (Director of the Regional Digital Imaging Center) helpfully and meticulously scanned all the pen and ink, pencil, and watercolor drawings from my sketchbooks. Bonnie Kern, Sahar Coston-Hardy, Abdallah Tabet, and Taylor Sim Burgess helped out in the early stages of this project. Particular gratitude and thanks are due to Kenneth Helphand for his early insight and advice. I'm indebted and have benefited immeasurably from the support, hard work, advice, and companionship of many who have worked closely with me over the past forty years: my partners, Robert Hanna, Dennis McGlade, Lucinda Sanders, Robert Bedell, Susan Weiler, Richard Roark, Hallie Boyce, Skip Graffam, Yue Li, Tiffany Beamer, Richard Newton, David Rubin, and associates at the time, Niall Kirkwood, Alistair McIntosh, Chris Allen, Allan Spulecki, Kate John-Alder, Les Bishop, and Sarah Williams. Additionally, a number of teachers and architects have each in their way been remarkable mentors—inspiring, provoking, and steering me toward ways to work and think about the human environment. These included Richard Haag, Victor Steinbrueck, Fred Bassetti, Ibsen Nelson, George Bartholick, Edward Larrabee Barnes, Joseph Passonneau, Peter Shepheard, and John Dixon Hunt. Alice Truax has, as always, been a remarkable editor in helping to produce and improve the final version of this work. Gordon Goff, Jake Anderson and Kirby Anderson, and their team at Applied Research + Design, an imprint of ORO Editions, have been as patient and gracious about my schedule as they have been superb in producing a finished book, with its graphic design by Pablo Mandel of Circular Studio. Finally, my devotion and gratitude to Victoria Steiger, whose encouragement, astute criticism, and support have sustained me through the many years and experiences related to my work, my thought, this book, and so much else.

Index

213